# PUDDINGS & DESSERTS

Edited by
Valerie Creek

# Contents

This edition first published 1980 by
Octopus Books Limited,
59 Grosvenor Street, London W1

©1980 Octopus Books Limited

ISBN 0 7064 1251 6

Produced and Printed in Hong Kong by
Manadrin Publishers Limited
22a Westlands Road, Quarry Bay

WALNUT AND RASPBERRY ROLL *(page 82)*
*(Photograph: Stork Cookery Service)*

# Weights and Measures

All measurements in this book are based on Imperial weights and measures, with American equivalents given in parenthesis.

Measurements in *weight* in the Imperial and American system are the same. Liquid measurements are different, and the following table shows the equivalents:

### Liquid measurements
| | |
|---|---|
| 1 Imperial pint | 20 fluid ounces |
| 1 American pint | 16 fluid ounces |
| 1 American cup | 8 fluid ounces |

Level spoon measurements are used in all the recipes.

### Spoon measurements
| | |
|---|---|
| 1 tablespoon (1T) | 15 ml |
| 1 teaspoon | 5 ml |

# INTRODUCTION

Whether it is mid-winter, which means steamed puddings are popular, or high-summer with its demand for ice creams, all these desserts and many more are given in this book. There are also cold and chilled desserts and desserts for special occasions or entertaining. For all those people in a hurry, there is a section of quick and easy desserts, which save time and are good for unexpected guests. To finish off there is a range of sauces, suitable for serving with any of the recipes in this book.

The dessert course gives the opportunity to introduce textures and flavours into the meal which are different from the previous courses. Try serving a crisp piece of shortbread or other biscuit (cookie) with a soft creamy pudding to give texture variation. Alternatively, a smooth sauce or lightly whipped cream poured over a crisp-textured pudding is also good.

If you are lucky enough to have a freezer, many of the desserts can be made ahead and frozen. Uncooked pastry doughs, rosettes of whipped double (heavy) cream, crumble toppings and sauces are all useful to have in the freezer and pancakes (crêpes) are particularly successful.

For some people, the dessert course of a meal is the best part, while for others it provides a pleasant finish to the meal as a whole. Whichever type you may be, there is something to suit your taste in this book.

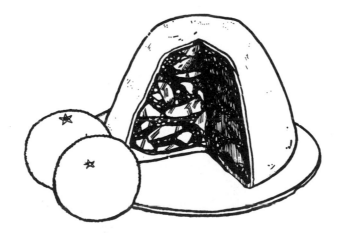

CRÈME BRÛLÉE *(page 58)*
*Photograph: British Egg Information Service*

# HOT PUDDINGS

## Dorset Treacle Tart

METRIC/IMPERIAL
**Pastry**
*225 g/8 oz plain flour*
*½ teaspoon salt*
*100 g/4 oz margarine*
*3 tablespoons water*
**Filling**
*5 tablespoons golden syrup*
*1 tablespoon black treacle*
*50 g/2 oz fresh breadcrumbs*
*1 medium cooking apple*
*50 g/2 oz mixed dried fruit*

AMERICAN
**Pastry**
*2 cups all-purpose flour*
*½ teaspoon salt*
*½ cup margarine*
*3 tablespoons water*
**Filling**
*5 tablespoons light corn syrup*
*1 tablespoon molasses*
*1 cup fresh breadcrumbs*
*1 medium cooking apple*
*⅓ cup mixed dried fruit*

Sift the flour and salt into a large bowl. Rub in the margarine until the mixture resembles fine breadcrumbs. Add the water and mix to a stiff dough. Knead lightly then roll out and use to line a 20 cm (8 inch) flan (pie) dish. Roll out the trimmings of pastry and cut into four strips, 25 cm (10 inches) long.

Place the syrup, treacle (molasses) and breadcrumbs in a bowl. Peel, core and finely chop the apple and add to the syrup, together with the mixed fruit. Mix thoroughly and pour the fruit mixture into the pastry case. Twist the strips of pastry and dampen the edges. Press on to the tart in a star design. Bake in a moderately hot oven (200°C/400°F, Gas Mark 6) for 35 to 40 minutes or until the pastry is golden and the filling heated through. Serve hot with Custard Sauce (see page 90) or ice cream.
**Serves 4–6**

# Lemon Meringue Pie

**METRIC/IMPERIAL**
**American pastry**
*150 g/5 oz margarine*
*225 g/8 oz plain flour, sifted*
*2 tablespoons water*
**Filling**
*4 tablespoons cornflour*
*300 ml/½ pint water*
*grated rind and juice of 1 lemon*
*225 g/8 oz caster sugar*
*2 eggs, separated*

**AMERICAN**
**Stirred pastry**
*⅔ cup margarine*
*2 cups all-purpose flour, sifted*
*2 tablespoons water*
**Filling**
*4 tablespoons cornstarch*
*1¼ cups water*
*grated rind and juice of 1 lemon*
*1 cup sugar*
*2 eggs, separated*

To make the pastry, place the margarine, 2 tablespoons of the flour and the water into a large bowl. Mix together until well blended, using a fork. Mix in the remaining flour to form a fairly soft dough. Turn on to a lightly floured board and knead until smooth. Rest for 30 minutes in a cold place. Roll out the pastry between two sheets of greaseproof (wax) paper and use to line a 20 cm (8 inch) flan ring (pie pan). Bake blind as for Peachy Meringue Trellis (page 15). Chill.

Place the cornflour (cornstarch), water, lemon rind and juice and 100 g/4 oz/½ cup of the caster sugar in a saucepan. Bring to the boil, whisking continuously, and simmer until the mixture thickens. Allow to cool slightly, then beat in the egg yolks. Pour the filling into the baked pastry case.

Whisk the egg whites until stiff, add most of the remaining sugar and continue whisking until glossy. Fold in the rest of the sugar and pile the meringue over the lemon mixture, making sure the filling is completely covered. Reduce the oven temperature to 150°C/300°F, Gas Mark 2 and bake for 20 to 30 minutes or until the meringue is crisp and a pale golden colour. Serve hot.
**Serves 6-8**

# Cherry Bakewell Tart

| METRIC/IMPERIAL | AMERICAN |
|---|---|
| *1 quantity of American pastry (see page 11)* | *1 quantity of stirred pastry (see page 11)* |
| **Filling** | **Filling** |
| *75 g/3 oz margarine* | *6 tablespoons margarine* |
| *75 g/3 oz caster sugar* | *6 tablespoons sugar* |
| *2 eggs, beaten* | *2 eggs, beaten* |
| *50 g/2 oz self raising flour* | *½ cup self-rising flour* |
| *50 g/2 oz ground almonds* | *½ cup ground almonds* |
| *few drops almond essence* | *few drops almond extract* |
| *100 g/4 oz glacé cherries, halved* | *½ cup halved candied cherries* |
| *2 tablespoons apricot jam* | *2 tablespoons apricot jam* |
| *little glacé icing* | *little glacé icing* |
| *few cherries and almonds to decorate* | *few cherries and almonds to decorate* |

Make one quantity of American (stirred) pastry as described on page 11. Chill for 30 minutes then roll out between sheets of greaseproof (wax) paper. Use to line a 20 cm (8 inch) flan tin (pie dish). Reserve any leftover pastry for decoration.

Place the margarine, sugar, eggs, flour, ground almonds and almond essence (extract) in a bowl and beat together until well mixed. (This should take about 2–3 minutes.) Spoon in the prepared pastry case and arrange the cherries on top. Decorate the tart with any remaining pastry, cut into strips. Bake in a moderate oven (180°C/350°F, Gas Mark 4) for 45 to 50 minutes. Remove the flan tin if using and glaze the top of the pie with heated apricot jam. Cool the pie slightly, then decorate with a little glacé icing drizzled over the top and a few extra cherries and almonds, if liked. Serve hot.
**Serves 6**

CHERRY BAKEWELL TART *(Photograph: Stork Cookery Service)*

# Apricot and Almond Tart

METRIC/IMPERIAL
1 x 425 g/15 oz can apricot halves,
  drained
1 x 18 cm/7 inch shortcrust pastry
  case, baked blind (see pages 15,
  16)
50 g/2 oz margarine
25 g/1 oz caster sugar
1 egg
1½ tablespoons golden syrup
25 g/1 oz self-raising flour, sifted
50 g/2 oz ground almonds

AMERICAN
1 x 1 lb can apricot halves, drained
1 x 7 inch basic pie dough pastry
  case, baked blind (see page 15,
  16)
¼ cup margarine
sugar
1 egg
1½ tablespoons light corn syrup
¼ cup self-rising flour
½ cup ground almonds

Place the fruit, hollow side down, over the base of the prepared
pastry case. Cream the margarine and sugar together. Beat in the
egg, then the syrup. Fold in the flour and ground almonds; mix
thoroughly. Spread the mixture over the apricots, and level the top.
Bake in a moderately hot oven (200°C/400°F, Gas Mark 6) for about
35 minutes or until the top is firm and golden. Serve hot.
**Serves 6**

# Apple and Ginger Pie

METRIC/IMPERIAL
1 quantity shortcrust pastry (see
  page 16)
**Filling**
500 g/1 lb cooking apples
50 g/2 oz sultanas
50 g/2 oz soft brown sugar
1 teaspoon ground ginger
2 tablespoons milk
little demerara sugar

AMERICAN
1 quantity basic pie dough
  (see page 16)
**Filling**
1 lb cooking apples
⅓ cup seedless white raisins
⅓ cup brown sugar
1 teaspoon ground ginger
2 tablespoons milk
little brown sugar

Roll out half the pastry and use to line an 18 cm (7 inch) pie dish.
    To make the filling, peel, core and slice the apples finely. Layer the
apple slices, sultanas (white raisins), sugar and ginger in the dish.
Roll out the remaining pastry to make a lid for the pie. Moisten the
pastry edges and press firmly together to seal. Trim away excess
pastry. Brush the top with milk and sprinkle with demerara (brown)
sugar. Make a few steam slits. Bake in a moderately hot oven
(200°C/400°F, Gas Mark 6) for 35 to 40 minutes or until the pastry is
evenly brown all over. Serve hot, with whipped cream or ice cream.
**Serves 4–6**

# Peachy Meringue Trellis

**METRIC/IMPERIAL**

**Pastry**
175 g/6 oz plain flour
pinch of salt
40 g/1 ½ oz margarine
3 tablespoons oil
1 tablespoon sugar
2 tablespoons water

**Filling**
1 tablespoon custard powder
300 ml/½ pint milk
3 tablespoons caster sugar
1 egg, separated
few drops vanilla essence
1 x 425 g/15 oz can sliced peaches,
  drained

**AMERICAN**

**Pastry**
1 ½ cups all-purpose flour
pinch of salt
3 tablespoons margarine
3 tablespoons oil
1 tablespoon sugar
2 tablespoons water

**Filling**
1 tablespoon custard powder
1 ¼ cups milk
3 tablespoons sugar
1 egg, separated
few drops vanilla extract
1 x 15 oz can sliced peaches,
  drained

To make the pastry, sift the flour and salt into a bowl. Rub in the margarine and oil until the mixture resembles fine breadcrumbs. Add the sugar and the water and mix to a firm dough. Roll out the pastry and use to line a 20 cm (8 inch) flan tin (pie pan). **Bake blind** by lining the flan case with a piece of greaseproof (wax) paper and filling with dried beans. Bake in a moderately hot oven (200°C/400°F, Gas Mark 6) for 15 to 20 minutes. Remove the beans and paper. Bake for a further 5 minutes then cool.

To make the filling, blend the custard powder with a little of the milk and 1 tablespoon of the sugar. Heat the rest of the milk and pour on to the custard cream. Return to the pan and bring to the boil, stirring continually, until thickened. Beat in the egg yolk and vanilla essence (extract). Cover and allow to cool. Whisk the cooled custard until creamy. Place in the prepared pastry case, and arrange the sliced peaches on top.

Whisk the egg white until stiff, add most of the remaining sugar and whisk again until glossy; fold in the rest of the sugar. Place the egg white mixture in a piping (pastry) bag fitted with a fluted nozzle. Pipe a trellis design over the surface. Return the pie to the oven for a further 5 minutes to brown the meringue. Serve hot.
**Serves 6**

# Syrup Tart

**METRIC/IMPERIAL**
**Shortcrust pastry**
*175 g/6 oz plain flour*
*pinch of salt*
*75 g/3 oz margarine*
*2-3 tablespoons water*
**Filling**
*225 g/8 oz golden syrup*
*25 g/1 oz butter*
*50 g/2 oz fresh breadcrumbs*
*grated rind and juice of 1 lemon*

**AMERICAN**
**Basic pie dough**
*1½ cups all-purpose flour*
*pinch of salt*
*6 tablespoons margarine*
*2-3 tablespoons water*
**Filling**
*¾ cup light corn syrup*
*2 tablespoons butter*
*1 cup fresh breadcrumbs*
*grated rind and juice of 1 lemon*

To make the pastry (dough), sift the flour and salt into a large bowl. Rub the margarine into the flour until the mixture resembles fine breadcrumbs. Add the water and mix to a firm dough. Knead on a lightly floured surface until smooth. Roll out and use to line a 20 cm (8 inch) pie plate. Trim and decorate the rim.

To make the filling, warm the syrup and butter together, then add the breadcrumbs, lemon rind and juice. Mix thoroughly together and pour into the pie plate. Bake in a moderately hot oven (200°C/400°F, Gas Mark 6) for about 30 minutes or until golden brown. Serve hot with custard sauce (see page 90), if liked.
**Serves 6**

# Custard Tartlets

**METRIC/IMPERIAL**
*175 g/6 oz plain flour*
*pinch of salt*
*75 g/3 oz margarine*
*3 tablespoons water*
*1 egg*
*1 x 450 g/16 oz can ready made
  custard*
*grated nutmeg*

**AMERICAN**
*1½ cups all-purpose flour*
*pinch of salt*
*6 tablespoons margarine*
*3 tablespoons water*
*1 egg*
*1 x 1 lb can ready made custard*
*grated nutmeg*

Sift the flour and salt into a bowl. Add the margarine and rub it into the flour until the mixture resembles fine breadcrumbs. Add the water and mix to a firm dough. Knead the dough lightly then roll out. Cut out rounds and use to line 15 to 18 patty tins.

Beat the egg and combine with the custard. Pour the mixture into the pastry cases, dividing it evenly between each case. Sprinkle a little nutmeg over each. Bake in a moderately hot oven (200°C/400°F, Gas Mark 6) for 25 to 30 minutes. Serve hot.
**Serves 6–8**

# Sugar Plum Pie

**METRIC/IMPERIAL**

**Pastry**
100 g/4 oz plain flour
pinch salt
75 g/3 oz butter
50 g/2 oz caster sugar
1 egg yolk
milk to mix

**Filling**
3 egg yolks
15 g/½ oz granulated sugar
300 ml/½ pint natural yogurt
½ teaspoon ground cinnamon
500 g/1 lb dessert plums, washed
25 g/1 oz blanched almonds
40 g/1½ oz demerara sugar

**AMERICAN**

**Pastry**
1 cup all-purpose flour
pinch of salt
6 tablespoons butter
¼ cup sugar
1 egg yolk
milk to mix

**Filling**
3 egg yolks
1 tablespoon sugar
1¼ cups unflavored yogurt
½ teaspoon ground cinnamon
1 lb dessert plums, washed
¼ cup blanched almonds
¼ cup brown sugar

To make the pastry, sift the flour and salt into a large bowl. Rub in the butter until the mixture resembles fine breadcrumbs; stir in the caster sugar. Combine the egg yolk with a little milk and stir into the flour mixture to form a firm dough. Roll out and use the pastry to line a greased 20 cm (8 inch) flan tin (pie pan).

For the filling, beat the egg yolks together, and add the granulated sugar, yogurt and cinnamon. Pour into the pastry case.

Cut the plums in half and remove the stones (pits). Place fruit, cut sides uppermost, in the custard. Bake in a moderately hot oven (200°C/400°F, Gas Mark 6) for 35 to 40 minutes. Place a halved blanched almond in each plum cavity, sprinkle with demerara (brown) sugar and return to the oven for a further 10 minutes to brown.

**Serves 6**

# Butterscotch Meringue Pie

| METRIC/IMPERIAL | AMERICAN |
|---|---|
| 50 g/2 oz plain flour | ½ cup all-purpose flour |
| 100 g/4 oz soft brown sugar | ⅔ cup brown sugar |
| 200 ml/⅓ pint milk | ⅞ cup milk |
| 50 g/2 oz butter | ¼ cup butter |
| 1 teaspoon vanilla essence | 1 teaspoon vanilla extract |
| 2 eggs, separated | 2 eggs, separated |
| 1 x 18 cm/7 inch shortcrust pastry case, baked blind (see pages 15, 16) | 1 x 7 inch basic pie dough pastry case, baked blind (see pages 15, 16) |
| 100 g/4 oz caster sugar | ½ cup sugar |

In a small pan, blend the flour with the brown sugar, then gradually stir in the milk. Bring to the boil, remove from the heat and add the butter and vanilla essence (extract). Beat the egg yolks into the slightly cooled mixture and pour into the prepared pastry case.

Whisk the egg whites until stiff and fold in half the caster sugar. Continue to whisk until glossy then fold in the remaining sugar. Pile the meringue roughly on top of the butterscotch filling, to cover and pull into peaks. Bake in a cool oven (140°C/275°F, Gas Mark 1) for 30 to 40 minutes or until golden brown. Serve hot, with pouring cream.
**Serves 6**

# Apple and Cheese Crumble

| METRIC/IMPERIAL | AMERICAN |
|---|---|
| 750 g/1½ lb cooking apples, peeled, cored and sliced | 1½ lb cooking apples, peeled, cored and sliced |
| 175 g/6 oz Cheddar cheese, grated | 1½ cups grated Cheddar cheese |
| ½ teaspoon ground cinnamon | ½ teaspoon ground cinnamon |
| 50 g/2 oz soft brown sugar | ⅓ cup brown sugar |
| 50 g/2 oz raisins | ⅓ cup raisins |
| 175 g/6 oz plain flour | 1½ cups all-purpose flour |
| 75 g/3 oz butter | 6 tablespoons butter |
| 50 g/2 oz caster sugar | ¼ cup sugar |

Grease a 600 ml/1 pint/2½ cup ovenproof pie dish. Peel, core and slice the apples and place in the dish. Sprinkle with 100 g/4 oz/1 cup of the cheese, the cinnamon, brown sugar and raisins. Sift the flour into a bowl. Rub in the butter until the mixture resembles fine breadcrumbs. Add the caster sugar and the remaining cheese. Mix together thoroughly.

Sprinkle the crumb topping over the filling. Bake in a moderately hot oven (200°C/400°F, Gas Mark 6) for 30 to 40 minutes or until the topping is crisp and a light golden brown. Serve hot with custard sauce or cream, if liked.
**Serves 4-6**

# Cherry Crumble Tarts

| METRIC/IMPERIAL | AMERICAN |
|---|---|
| 175 g/6 oz plain flour | 1½ cups all-purpose flour |
| 75 g/3 oz margarine | 6 tablespoons margarine |
| water to mix | water to mix |
| 1 x 425 g/15 oz can cherry pie filling | 1 x 15 oz can cherry pie filling |
| 1 tablespoon granulated sugar | 1 tablespoon sugar |
| 25 g/1 oz almonds, chopped | ¼ cup chopped almonds |

This may be cooked as a whole flan, using an 18 cm (7 inch) flan tin (pie pan) instead. Bake for about 30 minutes or until the pastry is cooked. Sift the flour into a bowl. Rub in the margarine, until the mixture resembles fine breadcrumbs. Take out approximately 25 g/1 oz/2 tablespoons of the crumbs and reserve. Add sufficient water to the remaining flour mixture and mix to a firm dough. Roll out and use the pastry to line 12 deep patty (tartlet) tins.

Place a generous spoonful of pie filling in each patty (tartlet) case. Add the sugar and chopped almonds to the reserved crumb mixture then sprinkle evenly over each patty (tartlet). Bake in a moderately hot oven (190°C/375°F, Gas Mark 5) for 15 to 20 minutes, or until the topping is crisp and golden. Remove from the tins and serve hot, with cream.

**Makes approx 12**

# Rhubarb and Raisin Charlotte

| METRIC/IMPERIAL | AMERICAN |
|---|---|
| 175 g/6 oz fresh breadcrumbs | 3 cups fresh breadcrumbs |
| 100 g/4 oz soft brown sugar | ⅔ cup brown sugar |
| 25 g/1 oz butter | 2 tablespoons butter |
| 1 x 425 g/15 oz can rhubarb, drained | 1 x 15 oz can rhubarb, drained |
| 100 g/4 oz seedless raisins | ⅔ cup pitted raisins |

Grease a 1.2 litre/2 pint/5 cup ovenproof dish. Cover the base with one third of the breadcrumbs and one third of the sugar. Dot with a little of the butter. Place half the rhubarb and raisins on top then layer with the remaining ingredients, finishing with a layer of crumbs and sugar. Dot with the remaining butter. Bake in a moderately hot oven (190°C/375°F, Gas Mark 5) for 40 minutes or until the top is golden and crisp.

**Serves 6**

*From rear clockwise:* RHUBARB AND RAISIN CHARLOTTE; CHOCOLATE AND BANANA PUDDING *(page 24)* SERVED WITH CHOCOLATE SAUCE *(page 90)*; PEACHY MERINGUE TRELLIS *(page 15)*; MINCEMEAT AND APPLE WHIRL *(page 31)* AND ST CLEMENT'S PANCAKES (CRÊPES) *(page 34)*.
*(Photograph: Flour Advisory Bureau)*

# Country Fruit Cobbler

| METRIC/IMPERIAL | AMERICAN |
|---|---|
| 1 kg/2 lb cooking apples | 2 lb cooking apples |
| sugar to taste | sugar to taste |
| 225 g/8 oz self-raising flour | 2 cups self-rising flour |
| pinch of salt | pinch of salt |
| 75 g/3 oz butter | 6 tablespoons butter |
| 15 g/½ oz caster sugar | 1 tablespoon sugar |
| 2 eggs | 2 eggs |
| ½ teaspoon ground cinnamon | ½ teaspoon ground cinnamon |
| 2 tablespoons golden syrup | 2 tablespoons light corn syrup |

Peel, core and slice the apples. Place the apples in a greased 20 cm (8 inch) pie dish. Sprinkle with sugar to taste and add enough water to just cover. Bake in a moderately hot oven (200°C/400°F, Gas Mark 6) for 10 minutes or until just soft.

Meanwhile, sift the flour and salt into a bowl. Rub in the butter and stir in the sugar. Add the beaten eggs and mix to a soft dough. Break off pieces of the scone dough and form into equal sized rolls. Place over the surface of the apple. Sprinkle with ground cinnamon and drizzle the syrup over the top. Return to the oven for a further 20 minutes or until the scones and apples have cooked. Serve hot with Custard Sauce (page 90) or pouring cream.
**Serves 6**

# Fiji Pudding

| METRIC/IMPERIAL | AMERICAN |
|---|---|
| 50 g/2 oz desiccated coconut | ½ cup shredded coconut |
| 150 ml/¼ pint milk | ⅔ cup milk |
| 100 g/4 oz golden syrup | 6 tablespoons light corn syrup |
| 100 g/4 oz butter | ½ cup butter |
| 100 g/4 oz caster sugar | ½ cup sugar |
| 2 eggs | 2 eggs |
| 175 g/6 oz self-raising flour | 1½ cups self-rising flour |

Place the coconut and milk in a small bowl and allow to stand. Grease a 1.2 litre/2 pint/5 cup basin and pour the syrup into the base. Cream the butter and sugar together until light and fluffy. Beat in the eggs, one at a time, then fold in the flour and finally the coconut. Mix thoroughly. Pour the mixture into the prepared basin, cover with greased greaseproof (wax) paper and tie securely. Bring a large pan of water to the boil and steam the pudding for 2½ hours, topping up with boiling water as necessary. Turn out and serve hot with Custard Sauce (page 90) if liked.
**Serves 6**

# Chocolate Cap Pudding

METRIC/IMPERIAL
*100 g/4 oz margarine*
*100 g/4 oz caster sugar*
*2 eggs*
*175 g/6 oz self-raising flour*
*pinch of salt*
*1 tablespoon coffee essence*
*1 tablespoon cooking chocolate*
  *drops*
*100 g/4 oz cooking chocolate*

AMERICAN
*½ cup margarine*
*½ cup sugar*
*2 eggs*
*1½ cups self-rising flour*
*pinch of salt*
*1 tablespoon strong black coffee*
*1 tablespoon cooking chocolate*
  *drops*
*4 squares semi-sweet chocolate*

Beat the margarine and sugar together until light and fluffy. Beat in the eggs, one at a time, beating well after each addition. Fold in the sifted flour and salt. Fold in the coffee essence (strong black coffee) and chocolate drops and mix thoroughly. Place the mixture in a greased 1.2 litre/2 pint/5 cup pudding basin, cover with greaseproof (wax) paper and tie securely with string. Bring a large saucepan of water to the boil and steam the pudding for 2 hours. Top up the water level with boiling water, when necessary.

Turn the pudding out on to a warmed plate. Slowly melt the chocolate, according to the packet directions, and pour over the pudding. Serve hot.
**Serves 6–8**

# Blackcurrant Castles

METRIC/IMPERIAL
*1 x 225 g/8 oz packet sponge*
  *pudding mix*
*1 x 275 g/10 oz can blackcurrants*
*2 teaspoons arrowroot*
*2 teaspoons honey*

AMERICAN
*1 x ½ lb packet sponge pudding*
  *mix*
*1 x 10 oz can blackcurrants*
*2 teaspoons arrowroot flour*
*2 teaspoons honey*

Grease about eight dariole moulds. Make up the sponge pudding mixture according to the packet directions. Half-fill each mould with the sponge mixture. Cover each with greaseproof paper and tie securely, steam for 45 minutes.

Sieve the blackcurrants and juice. Blend the arrowroot (flour) with a little water to make a thin cream. Heat the blackcurrant purée, pour a little over the creamed arrowroot, mix thoroughly and return to the pan. Bring to the boil, stirring continually. Add the honey and mix well. Turn the castle puddings out on to a warm flat plate and cover with the blackcurrant sauce. Serve hot.
**Serves 6–8**

# Bread and Butter Pudding

| METRIC/IMPERIAL | AMERICAN |
|---|---|
| 4 thin slices bread, buttered | 4 thin slices bread, buttered |
| 50 g/2 oz currants | 1/3 cup currants |
| 50 g/2 oz sultanas | 1/3 cup seedless white raisins |
| 50 g/2 oz caster sugar | 1/4 cup sugar |
| 450 ml/3/4 pint milk | 2 cups milk |
| 3 eggs | 3 eggs |
| few drops vanilla essence | few drops vanilla extract |
| grated nutmeg | grated nutmeg |

Cut the bread into neat triangles, and arrange alternate layers of bread, fruit and half of the sugar in a greased 1.2 litre/2 pint/5 cup ovenproof dish. Heat the milk in a pan, add the remaining sugar and heat until it has dissolved. Beat together the eggs and vanilla essence (extract), add the milk and strain into the dish. Leave to stand for 30 minutes. Sprinkle with a little nutmeg. Bake in a moderate oven (180°C/350°F, Gas Mark 4) for 45 to 50 minutes or until the custard has set and is a golden brown. Serve hot.
**Serves 4**

# Chocolate and Banana Pudding

| METRIC/IMPERIAL | AMERICAN |
|---|---|
| 100 g/4 oz self-raising flour | 1 cup self-rising flour |
| 15 g/1/2 oz cocoa powder | 2-3 tablespoons unsweetened cocoa |
| 100 g/4 oz margarine | 1/2 cup margarine |
| 100 g/4 oz caster sugar | 1/2 cup sugar |
| 2 eggs, beaten | 2 eggs, beaten |
| 2 ripe bananas, sliced | 2 ripe bananas, sliced |
| Chocolate Sauce (see page 90) | Chocolate Sauce (see page 90) |

Sift the flour and cocoa into a bowl. Cream the margarine and sugar together until light and fluffy. Gradually beat in the eggs, beating well after each addition. Fold in the flour, stir in the sliced bananas and mix thoroughly. Place in a well greased 900 ml/1 1/2 pint/3 3/4 cup pudding basin. Cover with greaseproof (wax) paper, tie securely then steam for 2 hours. Turn out on to a warm plate and serve with the prepared Chocolate Sauce. Serve hot.
**Serves 6**

BREAD AND BUTTER PUDDING
(Photograph: Flour Advisory Bureau)

# Baked Apples

METRIC/IMPERIAL
*4 cooking apples*
*3 tablespoons golden syrup*
*50 g/2 oz sultanas*
*grated rind of ½ lemon*

AMERICAN
*4 cooking apples*
*3 tablespoons maple syrup*
*⅓ cup seedless white raisins*
*grated rind of ½ lemon*

Wash and core the apples. Score the skin around the centre of each apple. Mix together the syrup, sultanas (white raisins) and lemon rind thoroughly and use to tightly pack the cavity in each apple. Place the apples in a shallow ovenproof dish and bake in a moderate oven (180°C/350°F, Gas Mark 4) for 25 to 30 minutes. Serve hot with pouring cream or Custard Sauce (page 90).
**Serves 4**

# Fluffy Meringue Apples

METRIC/IMPERIAL
*3 large cooking apples*
*100 g/4 oz granulated sugar*
*150 ml/¼ pint water*
*2 eggs, separated*
*175 g/6 oz caster sugar*
*175 g/6 oz cream cheese, beaten*
*25 g/1 oz flaked almonds*

AMERICAN
*3 large cooking apples*
*½ cup sugar*
*⅔ cup water*
*2 eggs, separated*
*¾ cup sugar*
*¾ cup cream cheese, beaten*
*¼ cup slivered almonds*

Peel and halve the apples then remove the cores. Dissolve the granulated sugar in the water over a low heat, bring to the boil and simmer for 1 minute. Add the apple halves and poach for about 10 minutes or until tender. Remove the apples from the syrup and place them hollow-side up in a 1.2 litre/2 pint/5 cup ovenproof dish. Pour a little of the syrup into the cavity of each apple.

Beat the egg yolks and 50 g/2 oz/¼ cup of the caster sugar together until thick and light. Gradually beat in the cream cheese, beating well to avoid lumps. Pour over the apples.

Whisk the egg whites until stiff and add half of the remaining caster sugar. Continue to whisk until glossy then fold in the remaining sugar. Pile the meringue over the apples and sauce, making sure the filling is completely covered. Sprinkle the almonds over the surface. Bake in a moderate oven (180°C/350°F, Gas Mark 4) for 35 minutes or until the topping is crisp and a light golden brown.
**Serves 4–6**

# Coffee Apple Pudding

| METRIC/IMPERIAL | AMERICAN |
|---|---|
| 2 large cooking apples | 2 large cooking apples |
| 175 g/6 oz self-raising flour | 1½ cups self-rising flour |
| ½ teaspoon ground cinnamon | ½ teaspoon ground cinnamon |
| 75 g/3 oz margarine | 6 tablespoons margarine |
| 100 g/4 oz caster sugar | ½ cup sugar |
| 2 eggs | 2 eggs |
| 1 tablespoon coffee essence | 1 tablespoon strong black coffee |

Grease a 1.2 litre/2 pint/5 cup ovenproof dish. Peel, core and chop the apples. Place in a pan with sufficient water to cover. Cover the pan and cook until a pulp.

Sift the flour and ground cinnamon together. Cream the margarine and sugar together until light and fluffy. Add the eggs, one at a time, beating well after each addition. Mix the coffee essence (strong black coffee) into the apple pulp and gradually add to the creamed mixture, alternately with the flour. Place the mixture in the prepared dish and level the top. Bake in a moderate oven (180°C/350°F, Gas Mark 4) for 45 minutes, or until firm to the touch and golden brown. Serve hot.
**Serves 4–6**

# Lemon Apple Meringue

| METRIC/IMPERIAL | AMERICAN |
|---|---|
| 750 g/1½ lb cooking apples | 1½ lb cooking apples |
| 3 tablespoons lemon juice | 3 tablespoons lemon juice |
| 225 g/8 oz caster sugar | 1 cup sugar |
| 25 g/1 oz butter | 2 tablespoons butter |
| 2 eggs, separated | 2 eggs, separated |

Peel, core and slice the apples. Place in a pan with the lemon juice, 100 g/4 oz/½ cup of the sugar and the butter. Cover and cook slowly until the apples are pulpy. Beat in the egg yolks. Pour the mixture into a shallow 1.2 litre/2 pint/5 cup ovenproof dish.

Whisk the egg whites until stiff and fold in most of the remaining sugar. Continue whisking until the mixture is glossy, then fold in the remaining sugar. Pile the meringue on top of the apple purée, making sure the filling is completely covered. Bake in a moderate oven (180°C/350°F, Gas Mark 4) for 10 to 15 minutes or until the meringue is a light brown colour and firm to the touch. Serve hot.
**Serves 4–6**

# Soufflé Omelette Surprise

METRIC/IMPERIAL
*250 g/8 oz fresh raspberries or fresh*
*strawberries, sliced*
*2 tablespoons kirsch*
*50 g/2 oz caster sugar*
*1 x 18 cm/7 inch baked sponge cake*
*3 eggs, separated*
*3 teaspoons water*
*1 family block ice cream*

AMERICAN
*1/2 lb fresh raspberries or fresh*
*strawberries, sliced*
*2 tablespoons kirsch*
*1/4 cup sugar*
*1 x 7 inch baked sponge layer cake*
*3 eggs, separated*
*3 teaspoons water*
*1 family block ice cream*

Soak the fruit in the kirsch and 25 g/1 oz/2 tablespoons of the sugar. Place the sponge cake on an ovenproof serving plate and arrange the fruit on top.

Beat the egg yolks, water and remaining sugar together. Whisk the egg whites until stiff, then carefully fold into the egg yolk mixture.

Place the hard ice cream on top of the fruit and immediately cover with the soufflé omelette mixture, making sure that the ice cream is completely covered. Quickly place in a hot oven (220°C/425°F, Gas Mark 7) for about 3 minutes to set and lightly brown the topping. Serve immediately.
**Serves 6**

# Hot Cherry Soufflé

METRIC/IMPERIAL
*25 g/1 oz cornflour*
*200 ml/1/3 pint milk*
*grated rind and juice of 1 lemon*
*100 g/4 oz cream cheese*
*50 g/2 oz sugar*
*4 eggs, separated*
*1 x 425 g/15 oz can black cherries*
*25 g/1 oz icing sugar, sieved*

AMERICAN
*1/4 cup cornstarch*
*7/8 cup milk*
*grated rind and juice of 1 lemon*
*1/4 lb cream cheese*
*1/4 cup sugar*
*4 eggs, separated*
*1 x 15 oz can black cherries*
*1/4 cup confectioners' sugar, sieved*

Blend the cornflour (cornstarch) with the milk and place in a small pan. Cook, stirring continuously, until the sauce thickens. Remove from the heat. Stir in the lemon rind and juice, cream cheese, sugar and egg yolks; mix well together.

Whisk the egg whites until stiff and carefully fold into the sauce mixture. Place the drained cherries in a greased 1.2 litre/2 pint/5 cup soufflé or straight sided ovenproof dish, then top with the soufflé mixture. Bake in a moderately hot oven (190°C/375°F, Gas Mark 5) for 30 to 35 minutes. Serve immediately, dusted with the icing (confectioners') sugar.
**Serves 4–6**

SOUFFLÉ OMELETTE SURPRISE
*(Photograph: British Egg Information Service)*

# Plum and Almond Whirls

METRIC/IMPERIAL
*225 g/8 oz self-raising flour*
*pinch of salt*
*100 g/4 oz shredded suet*
*approx. 150 ml/¼ pint milk*
*175 g/6 oz plum jam*
*25 g/1 oz soft brown sugar*
*25 g/1 oz flaked almonds*

AMERICAN
*2 cups self-rising flour*
*pinch of salt*
*¾ cup shredded suet*
*approx. ⅔ cup milk*
*½ cup plum jelly*
*2 tablespoons brown sugar*
*¼ cup slivered almonds*

Sift the flour and salt into a bowl. Stir in the shredded suet and add enough milk to form a soft dough. Turn out on to a floured surface and knead lightly. Roll out to a 30 cm (12 inch) square. Spread the jam (jelly) over the pastry, to within 1 cm (½ inch) of the edges. Dampen the edges and roll up tightly, folding in the edges as you go. Cut into 10 or 12 slices and place them, cut side uppermost, in a greased 25 cm (10 inch) sandwich tin (layer cake pan). Bake in a moderately hot oven (200°C/400°F, Gas Mark 6) for about 15 minutes. Sprinkle with the brown sugar and almonds, and return to the oven for a further 10 minutes. Serve hot, with custard if liked.
**Serves 4–6**

# Caramel Queen of Puddings

METRIC/IMPERIAL
*75 g/3 oz golden syrup*
*15 g/½ oz butter*
*300 ml/½ pint milk*
*50 g/2 oz soft white breadcrumbs*
*2 eggs, separated*
*few drops vanilla essence*
*50 g/2 oz caster sugar*

AMERICAN
*4 tablespoons light corn syrup*
*1 tablespoon butter*
*1¼ cups milk*
*1 cup soft white breadcrumbs*
*2 eggs, separated*
*few drops vanilla extract*
*4 tablespoons sugar*

Melt the syrup and butter in a heavy based pan, then cook until a deep golden brown. Carefully add the milk and bring back to the boil, stirring continuously. Pour the mixture over the breadcrumbs, in a heatproof bowl, and allow to cool slightly. Beat in the egg yolks and vanilla essence (extract). Turn the mixture into a greased 1.2 litre/2 pint/5 cup pie dish and bake in a moderate oven (160°C/325°F, Gas Mark 3) for 30 minutes.

Whisk the egg whites until stiff and fold in half of the sugar. Continue to whisk until glossy, then fold in the remaining sugar. Pile the meringue on top of the pudding, to cover completely, and return to a cool oven (140°C/275°F, Gas Mark 1) for about 30 minutes until the topping is set and a light brown colour. Serve hot.
**Serves 4**

# Rhubarb Cake

| METRIC/IMPERIAL | AMERICAN |
|---|---|
| 500 g/1 lb fresh rhubarb | 1 lb fresh rhubarb |
| sugar to taste | sugar to taste |
| 75 g/3 oz butter | 6 tablespoons butter |
| 50 g/2 oz caster sugar | 1/4 cup sugar |
| 1 egg | 1 egg |
| 100 g/4 oz desiccated coconut | 1/4 lb shredded coconut |
| 25 g/1 oz flaked almonds | 1/4 cup slivered almonds |

Wash and slice the rhubarb. Simmer the rhubarb with sugar to taste and a little water until soft. Cream the butter and the sugar together, until light and fluffy. Gradually beat in the egg then fold in the coconut.

Place the rhubarb in a greased 1.2 litre/2 pint/5 cup ovenproof dish, and top with the coconut mixture; level the top. Scatter almonds over the surface. Bake in a moderately hot oven (190°C/375°F, Gas Mark 5) for 20 minutes or until the top is a light golden brown. Serve hot with whipped cream, if liked.

**Serves 6**

# Mincemeat and Apple Whirl

| METRIC/IMPERIAL | AMERICAN |
|---|---|
| 350 g/12 oz cooking apples | 3/4 lb cooking apples |
| 75 g/3 oz soft brown sugar | 1/2 cup brown sugar |
| 225 g/8 oz mincemeat | 1/2 lb mincemeat |
| 225 g/8 oz self-raising flour | 2 cups self-rising flour |
| pinch of salt | pinch of salt |
| 100 g/4 oz shredded suet | 1/4 lb shredded suet |
| 8 tablespoons milk | 8 tablespoons milk |

Peel, core and chop the apples and place in a bowl. Add most of the sugar and all the mincemeat and mix thoroughly together.

Sift the flour and salt into a bowl. Add the suet and mix well. Stir in the milk and mix to a soft dough. Turn out on to a floured surface and roll out to a 30 cm (12 inch) square. Spread the apple mixture over the pastry to within 1 cm (1/2 inch) of the edges. Moisten the edges with water and roll up fairly tightly, folding in the edges as you go. Place the roll, cut side uppermost, in a greased 25 cm (10 inch) sandwich tin (layer cake pan), bending round to fit. Brush with a little milk and sprinkle with the remaining sugar. Bake in a moderately hot oven (200°C/400°F, Gas Mark 6) for 25 to 30 minutes or until risen and golden brown. Serve hot with Custard Sauce (see page 90) or cream

**Serves 4-6**

# PANCAKES FOR PUDDING

## Basic Pancake (Crêpe) Batter

METRIC/IMPERIAL
100 g/4 oz plain flour
½ teaspoon salt
1 egg, lightly beaten
300 ml/½ pint milk
oil for frying

AMERICAN
1 cup all-purpose flour
½ teaspoon salt
1 egg, lightly beaten
1¼ cups milk
oil for frying

Sift the flour and salt into a bowl. Make a well in the centre of the flour. Break the egg into the well and add about one-third of the milk. Beat the egg and milk together, so that the flour gradually falls into the liquid. Add more milk as the batter becomes stiff, until all the milk has been incorporated. Rest the batter for 30 minutes, adding more milk if necessary to thin it down. Heat enough oil to cover the base of an 18 cm (7 inch) frying pan (skillet). When the oil is ready, pour in enough batter to thinly coat the base of the pan (about 2 tablespoons). Cook gently until the base of the pancake (crêpe) is golden, turn over with a palette knife, or toss the pancake (crêpe) and cook the other side until golden. Slide the pancake (crêpe) on to a warm plate. Cook the remaining batter in the same way.

Makes approximately 8 pancakes (crêpes).

**Serves 4**

To keep the pancakes (crêpes) warm while the others are being cooked, place small sheets of greaseproof (wax) paper between each pancake (crêpe) and stack on a warm plate. Keep hot in the oven.

Pancakes (crêpes) can be made well in advance and stacked, as above, then stored in the refrigerator until use. Reheat by placing them, one at a time, in a hot, lightly greased frying pan (skillet). They will keep in the refrigerator for up to 5 days.

Pancakes (crêpes) can also be frozen. Stack as above, then pack in heavy duty foil or a polythene (plastic) bag. To reheat, either heat in a frying pan (skillet), or in a moderate oven (190°C/375°F, Gas Mark 5) for 20 to 30 minutes. They will keep in the freezer for up to 6 months.

PREPARED PANCAKES (CRÊPES) READY FOR FREEZING

# St. Clement's Pancakes (Crêpes)

| METRIC/IMPERIAL | AMERICAN |
|---|---|
| 100 g/4 oz butter | ½ cup butter |
| 50 g/2 oz icing sugar, sieved | ½ cup confectioners' sugar, sieved |
| 3 oranges | 3 oranges |
| grated rind and juice of ½ lemon | grated rind and juice of ½ lemon |
| 1 quantity cooked pancakes (see page 32) | 1 quantity cooked crêpes (see page 32) |

Melt the butter in a frying pan (skillet). Add the icing (confectioners') sugar and the grated rind and juice of 1 orange, and the lemon. Heat gently until the sauce simmers.

Remove the peel and pith from the remaining oranges. Divide into segments and chop the flesh. Divide the orange between the pancakes (crêpes) and fold up into cone shapes. Place in the pan of orange sauce; heat through. Serve hot, straight from the pan, with some of the sauce.
**Serves 4**


# Chocolate Banana Fold-ups

| METRIC/IMPERIAL | AMERICAN |
|---|---|
| 40 g/1 ½ oz butter | 3 tablespoons butter |
| 50 g/2 oz soft brown sugar | 2 tablespoons brown sugar |
| 2 tablespoons cocoa powder | 2 tablespoons unsweetened cocoa |
| 1 tablespoon golden syrup | 1 tablespoon light corn syrup |
| 2 bananas, sliced | 2 bananas, sliced |
| 1 quantity cooked pancakes (see page 32) | 1 quantity cooked crêpes (see page 32) |
| icing sugar | confectioners' sugar |

Melt the butter and sugar in a small pan, stir in the cocoa and syrup. Mix well then stir in the sliced bananas. Divide the filling between the pancakes (crêpes). Arrange the filling on one quarter of each. Fold the pancake (crêpe) over and over again, to form cone shapes. Place the pancakes (crêpes) on an ovenproof serving dish and heat through in a moderate oven (180°C/350°F, Gas Mark 4) for 5 to 10 minutes. Just before serving, dust with a little icing (confectioners') sugar. Pass any remaining banana filling separately. Serve hot.
**Serves 4**

# Orange Pancake (Crêpe) Rolls

METRIC/IMPERIAL
1 quantity cooked pancakes
175 g/6 oz cream cheese
2 tablespoons top of milk
3 tablespoons clear honey
50 g/2 oz sultanas
grated rind and juice of 2 oranges
1 tablespoon arrowroot
2 tablespoons soft brown sugar
few orange twists, to decorate

AMERICAN
1 quantity cooked crêpes
¾ cup cream cheese
2 tablespoons top of milk
3 tablespoons clear honey
⅓ cup seedless white raisins
grated rind and juice of 2 oranges
1 tablespoon arrowroot flour
2 tablespoons brown sugar
few orange twists, to decorate

Make the pancakes (crêpes), as page 32, and keep warm. Mix the cream cheese, top of milk, 2 tablespoons honey, sultanas (seedless white raisins) and half of the grated orange rind together. Set aside.

Make up the orange juice to 300 ml/½ pint/1¼ cups with water. Place the remaining orange rind and arrowroot (flour) in a small pan and gradually blend in the orange juice. Stir in the sugar and remaining honey and bring to the boil over a moderate heat. Simmer for 2 minutes. Spread the cream cheese filling on to the hot pancakes (crêpes) and roll them up loosely. Arrange attractively on a serving plate and pour a little orange sauce over the top. Decorate with orange twists. Hand any remaining sauce separately.
**Serves 4**

# Banana Cream Pancakes (Crêpes)

METRIC/IMPERIAL
1 quantity cooked pancakes
  (see page 32)
3 large bananas
grated rind and juice of ½ lemon
40 g/1½ oz sugar
150 ml/¼ pint double cream
icing sugar

AMERICAN
1 quantity cooked crêpes
  (see page 32)
3 large bananas
grated rind and juice of ½ lemon
3 tablespoons sugar
⅔ cup heavy cream
confectioners' sugar

Keep the pancakes (crêpes) hot, as described on page 32. Mash the bananas with the lemon rind and juice and sugar. Whip the cream until thick and stir into the banana purée.

Divide the filling between the pancakes (crêpes), and either roll up loosely or fold over into cone shapes. Arrange on a hot serving dish and serve immediately dusted with icing (confectioners') sugar.
**Serves 4**

# Jimmy Jammy Pancakes (Crêpes)

METRIC/IMPERIAL
*1 quantity cooked pancakes*
*(see page 32)*
*1 sachet instant dessert topping*
*150 ml/¼ pint milk*
*1 tablespoon strawberry jam*

AMERICAN
*1 quantity cooked crêpes*
*(see page 32)*
*1 sachet instant dessert topping*
*⅔ cup milk*
*1 tablespoon strawberry jelly*

Keep the pancakes (crêpes) hot, as described on page 32.

Make up the instant dessert topping, using the milk and following the packet instructions. Stir in the strawberry jam (jelly). Divide the filling between the pancakes (crêpes). Roll or fold up loosely, and serve immediately.
**Serves 4**

# Festive Pancakes (Crêpes)

METRIC/IMPERIAL
*1 quantity cooked pancakes*
*(see page 32)*
*1 sachet instant dessert topping*
*150 ml/¼ pint milk*
*225 g/8 oz mincemeat*
*caster sugar to serve*

AMERICAN
*1 quantity cooked crêpes*
*(see page 32)*
*1 sachet instant dessert topping*
*⅔ cup milk*
*½ lb mincemeat*
*sugar to serve*

Keep the pancakes (crêpes) hot, as described on page 32.

Make up the instant dessert topping, using the milk and following the packet instructions. Spread approximately 1 tablespoon of mincemeat over each pancake (crêpe) then cover with the instant dessert topping. Roll or fold up the pancakes (crêpes) and arrange on a warm plate. Sprinkle the sugar over the top and serve hot.
**Serves 4**

FRENCH APPLE FLAN *(page 78)*

# Sweet Apple Stack

| METRIC/IMPERIAL | AMERICAN |
|---|---|
| 25 g/1 oz butter | 2 tablespoons butter |
| 750 g/1½ lb cooking apples, peeled, cored and sliced | 1½ lb cooking apples, peeled, cored and sliced |
| 50 g/2 oz sugar | ⅓ cup sugar |
| 25 g/1 oz flaked almonds, browned | ¼ cup browned slivered almonds |
| plum jam | plum jelly |
| 1 quantity cooked pancakes (see page 32) | 1 quantity cooked crêpes (see page 32) |

Melt the butter in a large pan. Add the prepared apples to the pan with about 1 tablespoon of water. Cover the pan and slowly cook until the apples are soft but still whole. Stir in the sugar and almonds reserving a few for decoration.

Spread the pancakes (crêpes) with plum jam (jelly), then layer in a stack with the apple mixture. Place on a heatproof serving plate, cover with foil and heat in a moderate oven (180°C/350°F, Gas Mark 4) for 5 to 10 minutes. Sprinkle the top with the remaining almonds. Serve hot.
**Serves 4**

# QUICK DESSERTS

## Strawberry Cheese Fool

METRIC/IMPERIAL
*500 g/1 lb ripe strawberries, washed and hulled*
*75 g/3 oz cream cheese*
*150 ml/¼ pint natural yogurt*
*sugar to taste*

AMERICAN
*1 lb ripe strawberries, washed and hulled*
*6 tablespoons cream cheese*
*⅔ cup unflavored yogurt*
*sugar to taste*

Sieve or purée the prepared strawberries in a blender. Beat the cream cheese and yogurt together and add the strawberry purée with sugar to taste. Place in 4 stemmed glasses, and chill thoroughly before serving.
**Serves 4**

## Sweet Tooths

METRIC/IMPERIAL
*4 slices white bread, crust removed*
*1 egg*
*1 tablespoon milk*
*few drops vanilla essence*
*1-2 tablespoons sugar*
*butter*
*raspberry jam*

AMERICAN
*4 slices white bread, crusts removed*
*1 egg*
*1 tablespoon milk*
*few drops vanilla extract*
*1-2 tablespoons sugar*
*butter*
*raspberry jelly*

Cut the bread slices into fingers. Beat the egg, milk and vanilla well together and pour into a saucer or shallow dish. Dip the bread fingers into the egg mixture, then into the sugar. Melt butter in a frying pan (skillet). Fry the bread on both sides until browned and crisp. Serve hot, spread with raspberry jam (jelly).
**Serves 4**

# Dessert Oranges

METRIC/IMPERIAL
4 large oranges
300 ml/¼ pint double cream
75 g/3 oz walnuts, chopped
50 g/2 oz glacé cherries, chopped
50 g/2 oz plain chocolate, grated
few drops Cointreau (optional)

AMERICAN
4 large oranges
1¼ cups heavy cream
¾ cup chopped walnuts
⅓ cup chopped candied cherries
2 squares semi-sweet chocolate, grated
few drops Cointreau (optional)

Cut a slice from the top of each orange. Using a sharp knife, remove most of the flesh carefully, leaving a large cavity in each orange. Chop the orange flesh and reserve 2 tablespoons of the juice. Place the flesh back in the oranges. Whip the cream until thick and add the reserved orange juice. Stir in the nuts, cherries, chocolate and Cointreau, if using.

Spoon the cream mixture into the orange shells and chill in the refrigerator. Serve chilled.
**Serves 4**

# Lemony French Bread

METRIC/IMPERIAL
4 slices bread (from a large white loaf)
butter for spreading
2 tablespoons lemon curd
2 eggs
4 tablespoons milk
grated rind of 1 lemon
50 g/2 oz butter
caster sugar for sprinkling

AMERICAN
4 slices bread (from a large white loaf)
butter for spreading
2 tablespoons lemon curd
2 eggs
4 tablespoons milk
grated rind of 1 lemon
¼ cup butter
sugar for sprinkling

Spread the bread with a little butter and sandwich together with the lemon curd. Beat the eggs, milk and lemon rind together and place in a saucer or shallow dish. Cut the sandwiches into triangles, dip each in the egg mixture, making sure that they have absorbed the mixture into the bread. Melt the butter in a frying pan (skillet). Fry the sandwiches quickly until crisp and golden brown. Sprinkle liberally with sugar, and serve hot, with natural (unflavored) yogurt if liked.
**Serves 4**

DESSERT ORANGES (Photograph: Dairy Produce Advisory Service of the Milk Marketing Board)

# Banana Fluff

| METRIC/IMPERIAL | AMERICAN |
|---|---|
| 4 bananas | 4 bananas |
| 2 teaspoons lemon juice | 2 teaspoons lemon juice |
| 1 tablespoon soft brown sugar | 1 tablespoon brown sugar |
| 150 ml/¼ pint double cream, whipped | ⅔ cup heavy cream, whipped |
| 2 egg whites | 2 egg whites |

Mash three of the bananas well with a fork. Stir through 1 teaspoon of the lemon juice. Add the sugar and mix together well. Fold the whipped cream into the banana mixture.

Whisk the egg whites until stiff and carefully fold into the banana mixture. Spoon the mixture into 4 glass dishes. Slice the remaining banana and sprinkle the rest of the lemon juice over to prevent discoloration. Arrange slices of banana on top of each dessert. Chill before serving.

**Serves 4**

# Fresh Fruit Medley

| METRIC/IMPERIAL | AMERICAN |
|---|---|
| 2 large oranges, peeled and segmented | 2 large oranges, peeled and segmented |
| 2 bananas, sliced | 2 bananas, sliced |
| 2 apples, cored and sliced | 2 apples, cored and sliced |
| few black grapes | few black grapes |
| few red cherries | few red cherries |
| little lemon juice | little lemon juice |
| 4 tablespoons golden syrup | 4 tablespoons maple syrup |
| orange squash | orange squash |
| Cointreau to taste | Cointreau to taste |

Prepare the fruits according to their type and sprinkle a little lemon juice over the cut surfaces of the bananas and apples. Place all the fruits in a large glass bowl and stir lightly to mix. Place the syrup in a small basin and thin it down with orange squash. Stir in enough Cointreau to taste. Pour the syrup over the fruits and baste well. Chill in the refrigerator, basting occasionally. Serve chilled with cream or ice cream if liked.

**Serves 4**

# Grapefruit Meringues

| METRIC/IMPERIAL | AMERICAN |
|---|---|
| 2 large grapefruit | 2 large grapefruit |
| brown sugar to taste | brown sugar to taste |
| 2 tablespoons kirsch | 2 tablespoons kirsch |
| 2 egg whites | 2 egg whites |
| 100 g/4 oz caster sugar | 1/2 cup sugar |
| 2 glacé cherries, halved | 2 candied cherries, halved |

Cut the grapefruit in half and remove the pips. Using a grapefruit knife, remove the flesh from the pith then segment and return to the peel 'shell'. Sprinkle with brown sugar to taste, add the kirsch. Leave in a cool place for 30 minutes.

Meanwhile, whisk the egg whites until stiff. Fold in most of the caster sugar and continue to whisk until the meringue is glossy. Fold in the remaining sugar. Pile the meringue on to each grapefruit, making soft peaks on the surface. Brown under a hot grill for about 5 minutes or until the meringue is crisp and golden. Top with a glacé (candied) cherry and serve hot.

**Serves 4**

# Swiss Fruit Delight

| METRIC/IMPERIAL | AMERICAN |
|---|---|
| 2 tablespoons rolled oats | 2 tablespoons rolled oats |
| 150 ml/1/4 pint natural yogurt | 2/3 cup unflavored yogurt |
| 2 bananas, sliced | 2 bananas, sliced |
| 2 oranges, segmented and chopped | 2 oranges, segmented and chopped |
| grated rind of 1 lemon | grated rind of 1 lemon |
| 100 g/4 oz grapes | 1/4 lb grapes |
| 1 red apple, chopped | 1 red apple, chopped |
| 2 teaspoons sugar | 2 teaspoons sugar |
| pouring cream, to serve | pouring cream, to serve |

Mix the rolled oats and yogurt together. Add the prepared fruit, reserving a few pieces for decoration, and the sugar. Mix together thoroughly. Place in serving bowls and chill. Just before serving pour over a little cream and top with the remaining fruit.

**Serves 4**

# Quick Raspberry Dessert

METRIC/IMPERIAL
*150 g/5 oz golden syrup*
*1 x 425 g/15 oz can creamed rice*
  *pudding*
*225 g/8 oz fresh raspberries*
*double cream, to decorate*

AMERICAN
*½ cup light corn syrup*
*1 x 15 oz can creamed rice pudding*
*½ lb fresh raspberries*
*heavy cream, to decorate*

Place 1 tablespoon of the syrup into the base of 4 coupe glasses. Place the remainder in a bowl and add the rice pudding and most of the raspberries, reserving a few of the best for decoration. Using a rotary or electric beater, beat the mixture well together. Pile into the glasses on top of the syrup, chill. Just before serving, whip the cream until thick. Place in a piping (pastry) bag, fitted with a fluted nozzle and decorate each dessert with a generous whirl of cream and top with the reserved raspberries.
**Serves 4**

# Gingered Pears

METRIC/IMPERIAL
*150 ml/¼ pint water*
*100 g/4 oz caster sugar*
*1 teaspoon ground ginger*
*few strips lemon rind*
*4 Conference pears*
*50 g/2 oz flaked almonds*

AMERICAN
*⅔ cup water*
*½ cup sugar*
*1 teaspoon ground ginger*
*few strips lemon rind*
*4 Bartlett pears*
*½ cup slivered almonds*

Combine the water, sugar, ginger and lemon rind in a saucepan. Bring to the boil and simmer for 1 minute. Peel the pears, leaving them whole, and with the stalks intact. Poach gently in the sugar syrup until tender, basting occasionally. Place the pears and syrup in a serving dish, remove the lemon rind and chill. Decorate with the flaked (slivered) almonds. If liked, serve with pouring cream or Chocolate Sauce (page 90).
**Serves 4**

ORANGES IN CARAMEL SAUCE *(page 51) (Photograph: Jaffa)*

# Grapefruit Grand Marnier

METRIC/IMPERIAL
*2 large grapefruit*
*4 tablespoons thin honey*
*2 tablespoons Grand Marnier*

AMERICAN
*2 large grapefruit*
*4 tablespoons thin honey*
*2 tablespoons Grand Marnier*

Cut the grapefruit in half and remove the pips. Using a grapefruit knife remove the flesh from the pith then segment and return to the peel 'shell'. Drizzle the honey over each half, then pour a little Grand Marnier over each. Allow to rest in a cool place for about 30 minutes. Place under a hot grill for about 5 minutes until the fruit is hot and the topping golden. Serve hot.
**Serves 4**

# Gooseberry Fool

METRIC/IMPERIAL
*450 ml/³⁄4 pint cold custard, freshly
  made or canned*
*500 g/1 lb cooked gooseberries,
  fresh or canned*
*sugar to taste*
*green colouring (optional)*

AMERICAN
*2 cups cold custard, freshly made or
  canned*
*1 lb cooked gooseberries, fresh or
  canned*
*sugar to taste*
*green coloring (optional)*

Place the custard in a bowl. Sieve the gooseberries, or purée in a blender. Add the purée to the custard with sugar to taste and green colouring if necessary. Chill. Serve with crisp biscuits (cookies).
**Serves 4**

# Yogurt Mallow

METRIC/IMPERIAL
*2 egg whites*
*50 g/2 oz caster sugar*
*150 ml/¼ pint carton
  fruit-flavoured yogurt*
*1 tablespoon toasted coconut*

AMERICAN
*2 egg whites*
*¼ cup sugar*
*²⁄3 cup fruit-flavored yogurt*
*1 tablespoon toasted coconut*

Whisk the egg whites until stiff then gradually whisk in the sugar. Carefully fold in the yogurt and spoon the mixture into 4 stemmed glasses. Sprinkle each with the toasted coconut. Serve immediately, with crisp shortbread fingers, if liked.
**Serves 4**

# Butterscotch Whip

METRIC/IMPERIAL
*150 g/5 oz golden syrup*
*25 g/1 oz butter*
*600 ml/1 pint milk*
*40 g/1½ oz cornflour*
*1 egg, separated*
*½ teaspoon vanilla essence*
*whipped cream, to decorate*

AMERICAN
*½ cup light corn syrup*
*2 tablespoons butter*
*2½ cups milk*
*2 tablespoons cornstarch*
*1 egg, separated*
*½ teaspoon vanilla extract*
*whipped cream, to decorate*

Place the syrup and butter in a heavy saucepan. Cook over a gentle heat until a rich golden brown. Slowly add 450 ml/¾ pint/2 cups of the milk, and stir over a gentle heat until well blended. Blend the cornflour (cornstarch) with the remaining milk and stir into the hot liquid. Bring to the boil, stirring constantly. Add the egg yolk and beat thoroughly. Cool the mixture and add the vanilla essence (extract). Whisk the egg white until stiff and carefully fold into the butterscotch mixture. Pour into 4 glasses and allow to chill thoroughly. Decorate the Butterscotch Whips with whipped cream.
**Serves 4**

# Cranberry Trifle

METRIC/IMPERIAL
*1 swiss roll*
*1 x 382 g/13½ oz jar cranberry*
 *jelly*
*4 tablespoons sherry*
*600 ml/1 pint cooled custard,*
 *freshly made or canned*
*300 ml/½ pint double cream,*
 *whipped*
*fresh orange slices*
*toasted flaked almonds*

AMERICAN
*1 jelly roll*
*1 x 13½ oz jar cranberry jelly*
*4 tablespoons sherry*
*2½ cups cooled, custard, freshly*
 *made or canned*
*1¼ cups heavy cream, whipped*
*fresh orange slices*
*toasted slivered almonds*

Cut the swiss (jelly) roll into thin slices. Arrange around the sides and base of a glass bowl. Add the cranberry jelly and sherry and allow to soak thoroughly into the cake. Pour over the custard and chill until serving time. Just before serving, decorate with whirls of whipped cream, small slices of orange and the almonds. Serve cold.
**Serves 4-6**

# COLD AND CHILLED DESSERTS

## Chocolate Mousse

| METRIC/IMPERIAL | AMERICAN |
| --- | --- |
| *100 g/4 oz plain chocolate* | *4 squares semi-sweet chocolate* |
| *4 teaspoons water* | *4 teaspoons water* |
| *4 eggs, separated* | *4 eggs, separated* |
| *chopped mixed nuts to decorate* | *chopped mixed nuts to decorate* |

Melt the chocolate in the water in a small basin over a pan of
simmering water. Beat the egg yolks into the melted chocolate.
Leave to cool. Whisk the egg whites until stiff, then carefully fold
into the chocolate mixture. Pour into small individual glasses or pots.
Allow to chill in the refrigerator before serving. Top with a few
chopped nuts and piped whipped cream, if liked. Serve chilled.
**Serves 4**

CHOCOLATE MOUSSE
*(Photograph: British Egg Information Service)*

# Dutch Chocolate Dessert

| METRIC/IMPERIAL | AMERICAN |
| --- | --- |
| *225 g/8 oz unsalted butter* | *1 cup sweet butter* |
| *100 g/4 oz caster sugar* | *½ cup sugar* |
| *225 g/8 oz plain chocolate* | *8 squares semi-sweet chocolate* |
| *1 x 440 g/15½ oz can unsweetened chestnut purée* | *1 x 15½ oz can unsweetened chestnut purée* |
| *few drops vanilla essence* | *few drops vanilla extract* |
| *150 ml/¼ pint milk* | *⅔ cup milk* |
| *2 teaspoons gelatine* | *2 teaspoons unflavored gelatin* |
| *1 x 200 g/7 oz can mandarin orange segments* | *1 x 7 oz can mandarin orange segments* |

Cream 100 g/4 oz/½ cup of the butter and the sugar together until light and fluffy. Break the chocolate into squares and place in a small heatproof basin, over a pan of hot water to melt. Allow to cool slightly, then stir through the creamed butter mixture with the chestnut purée. Mix thoroughly. Add vanilla essence (extract) to taste. Turn the mixture into a well greased and lined 450 g/1 lb loaf tin and refrigerate overnight.

Place the remaining butter, the milk and gelatine in a heatproof bowl over a pan of simmering water and heat gently until the butter has melted and the gelatine is dissolved. Beat thoroughly for one minute. Chill the 'cream' in the refrigerator for 2 to 3 hours. Turn out the dessert on to a serving dish. Whip the 'cream' again. Decorate the cake with rosettes of cream and the drained mandarin oranges. Serve chilled.

**Serves 8-10**

# Oranges in Caramel Sauce

METRIC/IMPERIAL
4 large oranges
100 g/4 oz caster sugar
4 tablespoons water
2 tablespoons Cointreau
4 slices canned pineapple
black grapes

AMERICAN
4 large oranges
½ cup sugar
4 tablespoons water
4 tablespoons Cointreau
4 slices canned pineapple
black grapes

Carefully pare the rind from the oranges keeping the pieces as long as possible. Finely shred the rind and place in a small pan. Cover with water, bring to the boil, then simmer for about 10 minutes until the rind is tender. Drain and discard the water.

Remove the pith from the fruit and thinly slice the oranges, removing pips (pits). Re-assemble the slices in their original shape and secure with wooden cocktail sticks (toothpicks). Place the oranges in a heatproof bowl, tightly packed together.

Place the sugar and water in a small heavy pan. Bring to the boil, stirring until the sugar has dissolved, then boil rapidly until a rich caramel colour. Remove from the heat and pour over the oranges in the dish. Cover the dish and allow to cool then refrigerate overnight.

The next day, add the Cointreau to the syrup. Stir well to mix thoroughly, then baste the oranges several times so that the syrup is absorbed by them. To serve, place each orange on a slice of pineapple in a serving dish. Decorate with the orange rind and grapes and pour the sauce over the top. Serve chilled with pouring cream if liked.
**Serves 4**

# Swiss Apple

| METRIC/IMPERIAL | AMERICAN |
|---|---|
| 500 g/1 lb cooking apples | 1 lb cooking apples |
| 100 g/4 oz caster sugar | ½ cup sugar |
| 300 ml/½ pint double cream | 1¼ cups heavy cream |
| 3 tablespoons golden syrup | 3 tablespoons maple syrup |
| 50 g/2 oz cornflakes | 2 cups cornflakes |

Peel, core and quarter the apples. Place in a medium pan and simmer with the sugar and a little water until pulpy. Beat until smooth, then divide between 4 serving dishes. Leave to cool. Whip the cream until thick and spread a thin layer over the apple in each dish. Warm the syrup and toss the cornflakes in it. When the flakes are well coated, sprinkle them over the top of the cream. Serve chilled.

**Serves 4–6**

# Dorset Apple Cake

| METRIC/IMPERIAL | AMERICAN |
|---|---|
| 500 g/1 lb cooking apples | 1 lb cooking apples |
| 100 g/4 oz self-raising flour | 1 cup self-rising flour |
| pinch of salt | pinch of salt |
| 50 g/2 oz butter or margarine | ¼ cup butter or margarine |
| 75 g/3 oz caster sugar | 6 tablespoons sugar |
| 2 eggs, beaten | 2 eggs, beaten |
| 150 ml/¼ pint single cream | ⅔ cup light cream |

Grease and line an 18 cm (7 inch) deep cake tin (springform pan). Peel, core and chop the apples into 1 cm (½ inch) pieces. Sift the flour and salt. Cream the butter and sugar until light and fluffy. Gradually beat in the eggs, one at a time. Fold in the sifted flour and finally the chopped apples. Turn the mixture into the prepared tin (pan). Bake in a moderate oven (180°C/350°F, Gas Mark 4) for about 30 to 35 minutes or until cooked when tested. Cool the cake in the tin (pan).

Chill the cake, cut into slices and serve with the cream.

**Serves 6–8**

SWISS APPLE (Photograph: Tate and Lyle)

# Strawberry Soufflé

METRIC/IMPERIAL
*500 g/1 lb fresh strawberries*
*2 tablespoons brandy*
*juice of 1 lemon*
*100 g/4 oz caster sugar*
*4 teaspoons gelatine*
*150 ml/1/4 pint hot water*
*300 ml/1/2 pint double cream*
*2 egg whites*

AMERICAN
*1 lb fresh strawberries*
*2 tablespoons brandy*
*juice of 1 lemon*
*1/2 cup sugar*
*4 teaspoons unflavored gelatin*
*2/3 cup hot water*
*1 1/4 cups heavy cream*
*2 egg whites*

Hull and slice the strawberries, place in a bowl reserving some for decoration and pour over the brandy. Marinate for about 1 hour and add the lemon juice and sugar. Prepare a 600 ml/1 pint/2 1/2 cup soufflé dish by tying a doubled piece of greaseproof (wax) paper around the dish, that stands about 5 cm (2 inches) above the rim. Grease the paper rim lightly.

Dissolve the gelatine in the hot water, cool and add to the strawberries. Chill until beginning to set. Whip 250 ml/8 fl oz/1 cup of the cream until thick and whisk the egg whites until stiff. Gently fold the egg whites and cream into the strawberry mixture.

Place the mixture into the prepared soufflé dish. Chill in the refrigerator until set. Just before serving, remove the paper collar carefully from around the dish. Decorate the top of the soufflé with whirls of the remaining whipped cream and some strawberry slices. Serve chilled.
**Serves 4-6**


# Flummery Drambuie

METRIC/IMPERIAL
*4 egg yolks*
*75 g/3 oz caster sugar*
*3 tablespoons Drambuie*
*200 ml/1/3 pint double cream,*
 *whipped*

AMERICAN
*4 egg yolks*
*6 tablespoons sugar*
*3 tablespoons Drambuie*
*2/3 cup heavy cream, whipped*

Place the egg yolks and sugar together in a double saucepan or in a heatproof bowl over a pan of simmering water. Beat well together until the mixture has thickened and doubled in volume. Add the Drambuie and continue to beat until the mixture becomes thick again. Cool. Add the whipped cream and combine well. Pour into 4 stemmed glasses and chill in the refrigerator. Serve chilled accompanied by shortbread fingers.
**Serves 4**

# Coffee Creme Mousse

METRIC/IMPERIAL
15 g/½ oz gelatine
3-4 tablespoons hot water
3 eggs, separated
50 g/2 oz caster sugar
2 tablespoons coffee essence
300 ml/½ pint double cream
few glacé cherries
few flaked almonds

AMERICAN
2 tablespoons unflavored gelatin
3-4 tablespoons hot water
3 eggs, separated
¼ cup sugar
2 tablespoons strong black coffee
1¼ cups heavy dream
few candied cherries
few slivered almonds

Dissolve the gelatine in the hot water then cool. Beat the egg yolks and sugar together until thick and creamy. Stir the coffee essence (strong black coffee) and gelatine into the egg yolk mixture. Whisk the egg whites until stiff, then carefully fold into the mixture. Whip 250 ml/8 fl oz/1 cup of the cream until thick and fold into the coffee mixture. Pour into a wetted 900 ml/1½ pint/3¾ cup jelly mould. Chill in the refrigerator until set.

Unmould on to a serving plate. Decorate with whirls of the remaining whipped cream and the glacé (candied) cherries and almonds. Serve chilled.
**Serves 4**

# Pots Au Citron

METRIC/IMPERIAL
1 x 500 g/16 oz can sweetened
  condensed milk
225 g/8 oz cream cheese
grated rind and juice of 2 lemons
2 egg whites
15 g/½ oz gelatine
3 tablespoons water
chopped mixed nuts

AMERICAN
1 x 1 lb can sweetened condensed
  milk
½ lb cream cheese
grated rind and juice of 2 lemons
2 egg whites
2 tablespoons unflavored gelatin
3 tablespoons water
chopped mixed nuts

Beat the condensed milk and cream cheese thoroughly in a large bowl. Add the grated rind and juice of the lemons and blend well. Whisk the egg whites until stiff, then carefully fold into the cheese mixture. Soak the gelatine in the water then dissolve over hot water; stir evenly through the cheese mixture. Pour into 4 small pots and place in the refrigerator to chill. Just before serving decorate with chopped nuts.
**Serves 4**

# Rum Babas

METRIC/IMPERIAL
25 g/1 oz fresh yeast
6 tablespoons lukewarm milk
225 g/8 oz plain flour
½ teaspoon salt
25 g/1 oz caster sugar
4 eggs, well beaten
100 g/4 oz softened butter
100 g/4 oz currants
4 tablespoons golden syrup
6 tablespoons water
2 tablespoons rum
3 tablespoons apricot jam
150 ml/¼ pint double cream,
  whipped
glacé cherries to decorate

AMERICAN
1 cake compressed yeast
6 tablespoons lukewarm milk
2 cups all-purpose flour
½ teaspoon salt
2 tablespoons sugar
4 eggs, well beaten
½ cup softened butter
¾ cup currants
4 tablespoons maple syrup
6 tablespoons water
2 tablespoons rum
3 tablespoons apricot jelly
⅔ cup heavy cream, whipped
candid cherries to decorate

Mix together the yeast with the milk and 50 g/2 oz/½ cup flour.
Leave to stand for 20 to 30 minutes or until frothy. Combine the
remaining flour with the salt, sugar, eggs, butter and currants. Beat
thoroughly for 5 minutes. Add the yeast mixture and beat well.
Grease about 8 dariole moulds and half-fill them with the yeast
mixture. Leave in a warm place until the dough has risen to fill
three-quarters of the moulds. Bake in a moderately hot oven
(200°C/400°F, Gas Mark 6) for 15 to 20 minutes. Turn out and cool.

Warm the syrup, 4 tablespoons of the water and the rum together.
Spoon over the babas and leave to soak.

Heat the jam (jelly) and remaining water together. Brush over the
surface of each baba and allow to cool. Just before serving decorate
the babas with whirls of the cream and top each with a halved
cherry. Serve chilled.
**Makes approximately 8**

RUM BABAS *(Photograph: Flour Advisory Bureau)*

# Creme Brûlée

| METRIC/IMPERIAL | AMERICAN |
|---|---|
| 6 egg yolks | 6 egg yolks |
| 75 g/3 oz caster sugar | 6 tablespoons sugar |
| 600 ml/1 pint double cream | 2½ cups heavy cream |
| 1 teaspoon vanilla essence | 1 teaspoon vanilla extract |

Beat the egg yolks and 25 g/1 oz/2 tablespoons of the sugar together. Heat the cream to scalding point then gradually beat on to the egg mixture. Stir in the vanilla essence (extract) and pour in to 4 individual ovenproof pots.

Stand the pots in a shallow baking dish containing hot water. Bake in a moderate oven (160°C/325°F, Gas Mark 3) for 25 to 30 minutes or until set. Remove from the oven and cool. Sprinkle the remaining sugar over the surface of each pot. Place under a hot grill (broiler) to caramellize the sugar topping. Chill before serving.

**Serves 4**

Note: The egg whites can be used for making meringues or fruit fools.

# Summer Pudding

| METRIC/IMPERIAL | AMERICAN |
|---|---|
| 750 g/1½ lb mixed soft fruits (raspberries, strawberries, currants etc) | 1½ lb mixed soft fruits (raspberries strawberries, currants etc) |
| 75 g/3 oz caster sugar | 6 tablespoons sugar |
| 3 tablespoons water | 3 tablespoons water |
| 1 small white sliced loaf | 1 small white sliced loaf |

Prepare and wash the fruit, place in a large pan with the sugar and water, bring to the boil then simmer for about 1 minute or until the fruits are soft. Allow to cool. Reserve a few spoonsful of the syrup.

Grease a 900 ml/1½ pint/3¾ cup pudding basin. Remove crusts from the bread, and cut the slices in half diagonally. Arrange the slices in the basin, pressing them well to the sides, making sure that the basin is completely lined. Fill the basin with the fruit then place the remaining slices of bread over the top to completely enclose the fruit. Stand a saucer on top and place a heavy weight on top. Refrigerate overnight. Just before serving, unmould the pudding onto a serving plate. If necessary drizzle the remaining syrup over any white spots remaining. Serve with whipped cream, yogurt or ice cream if liked.

**Serves 4-6**

# Butterscotch Cream Pie

**METRIC/IMPERIAL**
75 g/3 oz butter
2 tablespoons caster sugar
pinch of ground cinnamon
75 g/3 oz cornflakes, crushed
100 g/4 oz soft brown sugar
50 g/2 oz plain flour
450 ml/¾ pint milk
2 egg yolks, beaten
½ teaspoon vanilla essence
150 ml/¼ pint double cream,
  whipped
grated chocolate, to decorate

**AMERICAN**
6 tablespoons butter
2 tablespoons sugar
pinch of ground cinnamon
3 cups cornflakes, crushed
½ cup brown sugar
½ cup all-purpose flour
2 cups milk
2 egg yolks, beaten
½ teaspoon vanilla extract
⅔ cup heavy cream, whipped
grated chocolate, to decorate

Melt 50 g/2 oz/4 tablespoons of the butter. Stir in the caster sugar and ground cinnamon. Pour over the cornflakes and toss to mix evenly throughout. Press the cornflake mixture on to the base of a 20 cm (8 inch) flan (pie) dish. Bake in a moderately hot oven (200°C/400°F, Gas Mark 6) for about 10 minutes. Cool.

Meanwhile place the brown sugar, flour and milk in a saucepan. Bring to the boil, then simmer for about three minutes, stirring constantly, until the sauce has thickened. Remove from the heat, cool slightly then stir in the egg yolks. Stir in the remaining butter and vanilla essence (extract); allow to cool.

Pour the cooled butterscotch mixture into the prepared flan (pie) case. Decorate with the cream and grated chocolate and serve chilled.
**Serves 6**

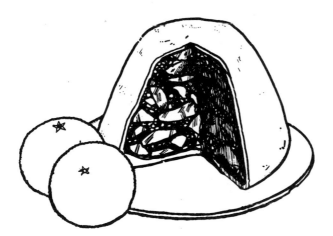

# Gooseberry Nut Whip

| METRIC/IMPERIAL | AMERICAN |
|---|---|
| 175 g/6 oz cream cheese | 3/4 cup cream cheese |
| 50 g/2 oz caster sugar | 1/2 cup sugar |
| 2 eggs, separated | 2 eggs, separated |
| 1 x 500 g/16 oz can gooseberries, drained | 1 x 1 lb can gooseberries, drained |
| 150 ml/1/4 pint double cream, whipped | 2/3 cup heavy cream, whipped |
| 50 g/2 oz hazelnuts, chopped | 1/4 cup chopped hazelnuts |

Blend the cream cheese and sugar together in a bowl until smooth. Gradually add the egg yolks, and beat thoroughly. Chop half the gooseberries and reserve the rest. Add the chopped gooseberries to the cream cheese mixture. Fold in most of the whipped cream, reserving a little for decoration. Whisk egg whites until stiff and fold in.

Sprinkle 25 g/1 oz/1 tablespoon of the nuts in the base of a large bowl. Pour half of the cream cheese mixture on top, then the whole gooseberries and end with the remaining cream cheese mixture. Decorate with a ring of the remaining chopped nuts and whirls of cream. Chill well before serving.
**Serves 4-6**

# Fruit Mousse

| METRIC/IMPERIAL | AMERICAN |
|---|---|
| 1 packet strawberry jelly | 1 packet strawberry flavored gelatin |
| 100 g/4 oz strawberries | 1/4 lb strawberries |
| 2 eggs, separated | 2 eggs, separated |
| 50 g/2 oz caster sugar | 1/2 cup sugar |
| 75 g/3 oz cream cheese | 6 tablespoons cream cheese |

Make up the jelly (gelatin) according to the directions on the packet, using only 300 ml/1/2 pint/1 1/4 cups water. Set aside to thicken. Crush or sieve the strawberries. Whisk the egg yolks and sugar together in a bowl over a pan of simmering water, until thick and pale coloured. Fold in the strawberries.

When the jelly (gelatin) has started to thicken, beat the cream cheese with a little of the jelly (gelatin) and add to the egg mixture, together with the rest of the jelly (gelatin). Whisk the egg whites until stiff and gently fold into the jelly (gelatin) mixture. Pour into individual glasses and allow to set. Serve chilled.
**Serves 4**

BLACK FOREST BOMBE *(page 67)*, FRUIT MOUSSE, GOOSEBERRY NUT WHIP *(Photograph: Kraft Foods Limited)*

# Magic Lemony Cheesecake

**METRIC/IMPERIAL**
*50 g/2 oz butter*
*2 tablespoons golden syrup*
*150 g/6 oz digestive biscuits,*
  *crushed*
*225 g/8 oz cream cheese*
*1 x 450 g/16 oz can condensed milk*
*120 ml/4 fl oz lemon juice*
*150 ml/¼ pint double cream,*
  *whipped*

**AMERICAN**
*¼ cup butter*
*2 tablespoons maple syrup*
*1½ cups crushed graham crackers*
*½ lb cream cheese*
*1 x 1 lb can condensed milk*
*½ cup lemon juice*
*⅔ cup heavy cream, whipped*

Line a 20 cm (8 inch) loose bottomed cake tin (pan) with foil. Melt the butter and syrup together. Stir in the biscuit (cracker) crumbs then press the mixture into the prepared tin (pan). Chill.

Beat the cream cheese in a bowl until soft then add the condensed milk and lemon juice. Mix thoroughly and pour into the prepared crumb base. Chill in the refrigerator for at least 1 hour. Just before serving, remove the cake tin (pan) remove the foil and slide the cheesecake on to a serving plate. Decorate with whirls of whipped cream. Serve chilled.
**Serves 6**

# ICE CREAM AND SORBETS

## Lemon Water Ice

METRIC/IMPERIAL
*2 generous tablespoons golden syrup*
*75 g/3 oz granulated sugar*
*450 ml/³/4 pint water*
*1 lemon*
*4 teaspoons gelatine*

AMERICAN
*2 generous tablespoons light corn or*
 *maple syrup*
*6 tablespoons sugar*
*2 cups water*
*1 lemon*
*4 teaspoons unflavored gelatin*

Place the syrup, sugar and 300 ml/½ pint/1¼ cups of the water in a medium pan. Add the thinly pared rind of the lemon and heat gently to dissolve the sugar. Bring to the boil, then simmer for about 5 minutes.

Meanwhile, dissolve the gelatine in the remaining water and the lemon juice; heat slowly until clear. Strain the syrup on to the gelatine mixture and allow to cool. Place in a freezer tray and freeze in a freezer of ice making compartment until thick and just beginning to set. Break down the ice crystals with a fork, then refreeze until completely set.

Serve with wafer biscuits (cookies), if liked.

**Serves 4**

# Minted Meringue Ice

METRIC/IMPERIAL
600 ml/1 pint milk
100 g/4 oz granulated sugar
½ teaspoon peppermint essence
2 egg whites
50 g/2 oz plain chocolate, chopped
fresh mint leaves

AMERICAN
2½ cups milk
½ cup sugar
½ teaspoon mint extract
2 egg whites
2 squares semi-sweet chocolate,
   chopped
fresh mint leaves

Heat the milk, sugar and peppermint essence (mint extract) together
in a medium pan to dissolve the sugar. Bring to the boil then leave to
cool. Pour into a plastic container and place in the freezer or ice
making compartment of the refrigerator until almost frozen.

Whisk the egg whites until stiff. Turn the ice into a large bowl and
whisk with a fork to break down the ice crystals. Fold in the whisked
egg whites carefully, then return the mixture to the plastic container
and refreeze until set.

When ready to serve, place spoonsful of the minted ice in tall
glasses. Scatter the chopped chocolate over the top and then top with
a few mint leaves. Crush the mint leaves, if liked, to release the
minty flavour.
**Serves 4**


# Coffee Sorbet

METRIC/IMPERIAL
600 ml/1 pint water
1 tablespoon caster sugar
1 tablespoon coffee essence
2 egg whites

AMERICAN
2½ cups water
1 tablespoon sugar
1 tablespoon strong black coffee
2 egg whites

Place the water and sugar in a medium pan and heat to dissolve the
sugar. Add the coffee essence (strong black coffee) and mix well.
Pour into a suitable freezer tray and freeze for 2 hours.

Turn the ice into a bowl and break down the ice crystals with a
fork. Whisk the egg whites until stiff and carefully fold into the
mushy ice. Pour into a 1.2 litre/2 pint/5 cup plastic container and
return to the freezer or refrigerator compartment for a further
2 hours or until frozen. Serve with sponge finger biscuits (cookies) or
shortbread.
**Serves 4-6**

MINTED MERINGUE ICE *(Photograph: The Dairy Produce
Advisory Service of the Milk Marketing Board)*

# Coffee Ice Cream Cake

METRIC/IMPERIAL
*2 eggs, separated*
*2 tablespoons coffee essence*
*50 g/2 oz icing sugar, sifted*
*150 ml/¼ pint double cream*
*1 x 18 cm/7 inch sponge cake*

AMERICAN
*2 eggs, separated*
*2 tablespoons strong black coffee*
*½ cup confectioners' sugar, sifted*
*⅔ cup heavy cream*
*1 x 7 inch sponge cake*

Whisk the egg yolks and coffee essence (strong black coffee) together until well blended. Whisk the egg whites until stiff. Add the icing (confectioners') sugar to egg whites, a tablespoon at a time, until it is all incorporated. Gradually add the egg yolk mixture to the egg white mixture. Lightly whip the cream and gently fold it into the egg mixture. Pour the mixture into a freezer tray and place in the freezer or ice making compartment of the refrigerator until frozen.

Just before serving, split the sponge cake into 3 layers. Divide the ice cream equally between the layers and re-assemble the cake. Dust with some extra icing (confectioners') sugar and serve immediately.
**Serves 4-6**

# Brown Bread Ice Cream

METRIC/IMPERIAL
*300 ml/½ pint double cream*
*150 ml/¼ pint single cream*
*75 g/3 oz icing sugar, sifted*
*100 g/4 oz brown breadcrumbs*
*2 eggs, separated*
*1 tablespoon dark rum (optional)*

AMERICAN
*1¼ cups heavy cream*
*⅔ cup light cream*
*¾ cup confectioners' sugar, sifted*
*2 cups brown breadcrumbs*
*2 eggs, separated*
*1 tablespoon dark rum (optional)*

Whip the double (heavy) cream until thick, then stir in the single (light) cream. Fold in the icing (confectioners') sugar and breadcrumbs. Blend the egg yolks and add the rum, if using, then carefully fold into the cream mixture. Whisk the egg whites until almost stiff, then fold them into the mixture. Pour into a freezer tray or rigid polythene (plastic) box. Place in the freezer or in the ice making compartment of the refrigerator and freeze until frozen. This ice cream does not require beating during freezing. Serve with fresh fruit and crisp biscuits.
**Serves 4-6**

# Black Forest Bombe

METRIC/IMPERIAL

**Chocolate Ice Cream**
175 g/6 oz cream cheese
90 g/3½ oz caster sugar
100 g/4 oz plain chocolate
250 ml/8 fl oz milk
150 ml/¼ pint double cream

**Cherry Ice Cream**
75 g/3 oz cream cheese
40 g/1½ oz caster sugar
65 ml/2½ fl oz milk
65 ml/2½ fl oz double cream
½ x 425 g/15 oz can cherry pie
 filling

**Plain Ice Cream**
75 g/3 oz cream cheese
40 g/1½ oz caster sugar
150 ml/¼ pint milk
2 tablespoons double cream

AMERICAN

**Chocolate Ice Cream**
¾ cup cream cheese
7 tablespoons sugar
4 squares semi-sweet chocolate
1 cup milk
⅔ cup heavy cream

**Cherry Ice Cream**
6 tablespoons cream cheese
3 tablespoons sugar
⅓ cup milk
⅓ cup heavy cream
½ x 15 oz can cherry pie filling

**Plain Ice Cream**
6 tablespoons cream cheese
3 tablespoons sugar
⅔ cup milk
2 tablespoons heavy cream

To make the Chocolate Ice Cream, blend together the cream cheese and sugar until smooth. Melt the chocolate in a heatproof basin over a pan of hot water, cool slightly, then add to the cream cheese mixture. Gradually beat in the milk and cream and pour into a freezer tray. Freeze for approximately 40 minutes.

To make the Cherry Ice Cream, blend together the cream cheese and sugar until smooth. Gradually beat in the milk, cream and half the can of pie filling. Mix well together. Pour into a freezer tray and freeze for about 40 minutes.

Make the Plain Ice Cream, following the Chocolate Ice Cream method and omitting the flavouring. Pour into a freezer tray and freeze in the freezer or ice making compartment of the refrigerator for 40 minutes.

Thoroughly chill a 15 cm (6 inch) loose bottomed cake tin (springform pan). Cover the base and sides of the chilled tin (pan) with the chocolate ice cream mixture, return to the freezer for about 15 minutes. Next, use the cherry ice cream to line the chocolate ice cream, as above. Return the tin (pan) to the freezer to firm up.

Finally fill the centre cavity with the plain ice cream and any remaining cherry ice cream. Return the ice cream to the freezer for about 1½-2 hours. When ready to serve, quickly dip the tin (pan) in a bowl of hot water, to loosen the ice cream. Turn the Black Forest Bombe on to a serving plate and serve immediately with cream.
**Serves 6-8**

# DESSERTS FOR SPECIAL OCCASIONS

## Champagne Jelly

A delicious dessert for a really special occasion such as a wedding, christening or anniversary.

METRIC/IMPERIAL
5 teaspoons gelatine
120 ml/4 fl oz hot water
50 g/2 oz caster sugar
1 bottle champagne or sparkling
  white wine
  (approx 750 ml/26 fl oz)
green grapes
1 egg white, lightly beaten
a little extra caster sugar

AMERICAN
5 teaspoons unflavored gelatin
1/2 cup hot water
1/4 cup sugar
1 bottle champagne or sparkling
  white wine (approx 26 fl oz)
green grapes
1 egg white, lightly beaten
a little extra sugar

Place the gelatine in a small bowl and pour on the hot water, stir briskly until dissolved. Add the sugar and stir again, until dissolved. Pour the syrup into a large bowl and allow it to cool. Carefully uncork the champagne or wine and stir into the gelatine mixture. The mixture will froth up, remove the froth (this may be used as a flavour in a parfait). Pour the champagne jelly into stemmed glasses and place in the refrigerator to set. Just before serving, dip the grapes into the egg white and immediately into a little sugar. Allow to dry then place the sugared grapes on top of each glass.
**Serves 4-6**

CHAMPAGNE JELLY (*Photograph: Davis Gelatine Limited*)

# Port Wine Soufflé

METRIC/IMPERIAL
*3 teaspoons gelatine*
*5 tablespoons hot water*
*2 eggs, separated*
*50 g/2 oz sugar*
*200 ml/⅓ pint milk, heated*
*5 tablespoons port wine*
*red colouring (optional)*
*150 ml/¼ pint double cream,*
  *whipped*

AMERICAN
*3 teaspoons unflavored gelatin*
*5 tablespoons hot water*
*2 eggs, separated*
*¼ cup sugar*
*⅞ cup milk, heated*
*5 tablespoons port wine*
*red coloring (optional)*
*⅔ cup heavy cream, whipped*

Prepare a 15 cm (6 inch) soufflé dish by tying a double band of greaseproof (wax) paper around the dish that extends about 5 cm (2 inches) above the rim. Lightly grease the inside edge of the paper.

Dissolve the gelatine in the hot water. Allow to cool. Whisk the egg yolks and sugar together in a large bowl until thick and creamy. Gradually add the hot milk stirring until the sugar is dissolved, then cool. Add the cooled gelatine and mix thoroughly. Add the port wine and some red colouring, if necessary, to give a pink colour. Refrigerate until the mixture starts to thicken. Fold in most of the whipped cream, reserving a little for decoration. Whisk the egg whites until stiff and fold carefully into the mixture. Pour into the prepared soufflé dish. Chill in the refrigerator. Just before serving, remove the paper band and decorate with the reserved cream.
**Serves 4-6**

# Valentine Pineapple Cream

METRIC/IMPERIAL
*1 x 400 g/14 oz can pineapple*
  *chunks*
*3 teaspoons gelatine*
*75 g/3 oz Edam cheese, grated*
*2 egg yolks*
*50 g/2 oz caster sugar*
*200 ml/⅓ pint double cream*
*few pineapple rings*

AMERICAN
*1 x 14 oz can pineapple chunks*
*3 teaspoons unflavored gelatin*
*¾ cup grated Edam cheese*
*2 egg yolks*
*¼ cup sugar*
*⅞ cup heavy cream*
*few pineapple rings*

Drain the pineapple chunks and heat the juice in a small pan. Add the juice to the gelatine and stir until the gelatine has dissolved. Place the gelatine in a blender. Add the pineapple chunks, cheese, egg yolks and sugar, and blend until smooth. Turn into a mixing bowl. Whisk the cream until thick and fold into the pineapple mixture. Pour into a 900 ml/1½ pint/3¾ cup mould, preferably heart-shaped. Refrigerate until set. Unmould and decorate with the pineapple rings.
**Serves 6**

# Chocolate Fondue

| METRIC/IMPERIAL | AMERICAN |
|---|---|
| 40 g/1 ½ oz cornflour | ⅓ cup cornstarch |
| 2 tablespoons sugar | 2 tablespoons sugar |
| 600 ml/1 pint milk | 2 ½ cups milk |
| 100 g/4 oz plain chocolate, roughly chopped | 4 squares semi-sweet chocolate, roughly chopped |
| **To serve** | **To serve** |
| banana pieces | banana pieces |
| Turkish Delight | Turkish Delight |
| marshmallows | marshmallows |
| orange segments | orange segments |
| grapes | grapes |
| apple pieces | apple pieces |
| sponge cake cubes | sponge cake cubes |

Blend the cornflour (cornstarch) and sugar to a smooth paste with a little of the milk. Heat the remaining milk add the cornflour (cornstarch) mixture and slowly bring to the boil, stirring continuously. Simmer for 1 minute. Reduce the heat as low as possible and add the chocolate. Stir occasionally until the sauce is smooth and all the chocolate has melted. Pour into a fondue pot or other pretty heatproof dish and serve hot. Arrange the fruit, etc, on a serving platter with cocktail sticks (toothpicks). The guests can help themselves then dip the chosen food into the sauce.
**Serves 4-6**

# Grape Whisper

| METRIC/IMPERIAL | AMERICAN |
|---|---|
| 225 g/8 oz green and black grapes, washed, halved and pipped | ½ lb green and black grapes, washed, halved and pitted |
| 1 ½ tablespoons white wine | 1 ½ tablespoons white wine |
| 3 egg whites | 3 egg whites |
| 75 g/3 oz caster sugar | 6 tablespoons sugar |
| crisp biscuits, to serve | crisp cookies, to serve |

Halve the grapes and remove the pips (pits). Marinate in the wine for about an hour, turning from time to time. Whisk the egg whites until stiff then gradually whisk in the sugar. Carefully fold in the grapes. Spoon the mixture into stemmed glasses and serve immediately, accompanied by crisp biscuits (cookies).
**Serves 4**

# Crispy Fruit Fritters

These fritters, called Oliebollen, are a traditional Dutch New Year's Eve delicacy.

| METRIC/IMPERIAL | AMERICAN |
|---|---|
| *300 ml/½ pint lukewarm milk* | *1¼ cups lukewarm milk* |
| *15 g/½ oz fresh yeast or* | *½ oz compressed yeast or* |
| *2 teaspoons dried yeast* | *2 teaspoons dried yeast* |
| *1 teaspoon sugar* | *1 teaspoon sugar* |
| *450 g/1 lb plain flour* | *4 cups all-purpose flour* |
| *salt* | *salt* |
| *2 eggs* | *2 eggs* |
| *225 g/8 oz currants* | *½ lb currants* |
| *50 g/2 oz candied peel* | *⅓ cup candied peel* |
| *1 small apple, cored and chopped* | *1 small apple, cored and chopped* |
| *oil for deep-frying* | *oil for deep-frying* |
| *icing sugar* | *confectioners' sugar* |

Add a little of the lukewarm milk to the yeast with the teaspoon of sugar. Set aside in a warm place for about 20 minutes or until the dried yeast mixture begins to bubble.

Sift the flour and salt together. Add the remaining milk, the yeast mixture, beaten eggs, currants, candied peel and apple. Mix well until a dough is formed. Turn on to a floured surface and knead the dough thoroughly until smooth and elastic. Leave in a covered bowl in a warm place for about 1 hour or until doubled in bulk.

Heat the oil in a deep pan. Using two greased dessertspoons, place small spoonsful of the mixture into the hot oil and fry until golden brown, turning when necessary. Drain the fritters on absorbent kitchen paper and dust with icing (confectioners') sugar. Serve hot.
**Serves 6-8**

CRISPY FRUIT FRITTERS *(Photograph: Dutch Dairy Bureau)*

# Profiteroles with Apple and Blackberry Sauce

METRIC/IMPERIAL
1 quantity of choux pastry
 (see page 80)
**Filling**
75 g/3 oz cream cheese
3 tablespoons natural yogurt
sugar to taste
**Sauce**
250 g/8 oz blackberries
250 g/8 oz cooking apples
sugar to taste

AMERICAN
1 quantity of choux pastry
 (see page 80)
**Filling**
6 tablespoons cream cheese
3 tablespoons unflavored yogurt
sugar to taste
**Sauce**
½ lb blackberries
½ lb cooking apples
sugar to taste

Make the choux pastry as described on page 80. Place small spoonsful of the mixture or pipe small balls on to a greased baking tray. Bake in a moderately hot oven (200°C/400°F, Gas Mark 6) for 15 to 20 minutes, or until puffy and golden brown. Slit each puff to allow the steam to escape. Cool.

To make the filling, blend the cream cheese with the yogurt and add sugar to taste. Place a little of the cheese mixture in the centre of each puff. Pile the profiteroles on to a serving dish.

To make sauce, wash blackberries and pick over. Peel, core and chop the apples and cook with the blackberries in a pan with a little water until tender. Beat the fruit down to form a sauce, and add sugar to taste. Pour the sauce over the profiteroles to serve. This can be served hot or cold.
**Serves 4-6**

# Tipsy Peaches

METRIC/IMPERIAL
1 x 425 g/15 oz can peach halves,
 drained
75 g/3 oz cream cheese
3 digestive biscuits, crushed
25 g/1 oz ground almonds
120 ml/4 fl oz white wine or cider

AMERICAN
1 x 15 oz can peach halves,
 drained
6 tablespoons cream cheese
3 graham crackers, crushed
¼ cup ground almonds
½ cup white wine or hard cider

Place the peaches, hollow side up, in a shallow ovenproof dish. Mix the cream cheese, crumbs and ground almonds together. Place a little of the crumb mixture in each peach hollow. Pour the wine or cider around the peaches. Bake in a moderate oven (180°C/350°F, Gas Mark 4) for 10 to 15 minutes. Serve hot or cold.
**Serves 4**

# Danish Rum Cake

**METRIC/IMPERIAL**
*65 g/2½ oz unsalted butter*
*65 g/2½ oz plain flour*
*7 g/¼ oz yeast*
*3 tablespoons single cream*
*1 teaspoon sugar*
*2 eggs*
**Syrup**
*100 g/4 oz caster sugar*
*150 ml/¼ pint boiling water*
*3 tablespoons rum*
**Decoration**
*mixed fruit, fresh or canned*
*150 ml/¼ pint double cream,*
  *whipped*

**AMERICAN**
*5 tablespoons sweet butter*
*½ cup plus 2 tablespoons*
  *all-purpose flour*
*¼ oz compressed yeast*
*3 tablespoons light cream*
*1 teaspoon sugar*
*2 eggs*
**Syrup**
*½ cup sugar*
*⅔ cup boiling water*
*3 tablespoons rum*
**Decoration**
*mixed fruit, fresh or canned*
*⅔ cup heavy cream, whipped*

Rub the butter into the flour until the mixture resembles fine breadcrumbs. Mix the yeast with the cream and the teaspoon of sugar. Add to the flour together with the beaten eggs. Beat the dough thoroughly. Pour into a greased ring mould and leave to prove in a warm place for about 30 minutes. Bake in a moderately hot oven (200°C/400°F, Gas Mark 6) for about 30 minutes or until cooked when tested. Cool.

About 1 hour before serving, place the cake on a serving dish.

For the syrup, dissolve the sugar in a thick pan. Add the boiling water and simmer rapidly until the syrup thickens. Add the rum and cool slightly. Sprinkle the syrup on to the cake and leave to stand for 30 minutes. Fill the centre of the cake with fruit either in season or canned and decorate with whipped cream. Serve chilled.

**Serves 4–6**

# Lemon and Walnut Cheesecake

METRIC/IMPERIAL
500 g/1 lb cottage cheese, sieved
grated rind and juice of 2 lemons
3 teaspons gelatine
4 tablespoons hot water
2 eggs, separated
100 g/4 oz caster sugar
300 ml/½ pint double cream
175 g/6 oz digestive biscuits,
  crushed
75 g/3 oz butter, melted
few walnut halves

AMERICAN
2 cups cottage cheese, sieved
grated rind and juice of 2 lemons
3 teaspoons unflavored gelatin
4 tablespoons hot water
2 eggs, separated
½ cup sugar
1¼ cup heavy cream
2¼ cups crushed graham crackers
6 tablespoons butter, melted
few walnut halves

Grease a 20 cm (8 inch) loose bottomed cake tin (pan). Blend the cottage cheese, lemon rind and juice together. Place the gelatine in a small bowl with the hot water and stir until it has dissolved. Mix the egg yolks and sugar together until thick, then add to the gelatine. Heat over hot water until the mixture thickens slightly. Cool and add to the cottage cheese. When the mixture is on the point of setting, fold in 150 ml/¼ pint/⅔ cup of the cream, whipped, and the whisked egg whites. Pour into the tin (pan) and chill in the refrigerator.

Mix together the biscuit (cracker) crumbs and melted butter and spread over the cheesecake. Press lightly so the crumbs will stick together. Allow to set. Turn out on to a serving plate, decorate with whipped cream and walnuts, then serve.
**Serves 8–10**

# Cranberry Sherry Mousse

This is an ideal dessert for Boxing Day, as the ingredients can usually be found in the cupboard at Christmas. It is deliciously light sweet to follow all the richer foods of Christmas Day.

METRIC/IMPERIAL
1 x 382 g/13½ oz jar
  cranberry jelly
4 tablespoons dry sherry
150 ml/¼ pint double cream
25 g/1 oz walnuts, chopped

AMERICAN
1 x 13½ oz jar cranberry jelly
4 tablespoons dry sherry
⅔ cup heavy cream
¼ cup chopped walnuts

Place the jelly in a bowl, add the sherry and whisk well together. Gently fold in the whipped cream and pile into individual glasses. Decorate with the chopped nuts and serve chilled.
**Serves 4**

LEMON AND WALNUT CHEESECAKE (Photograph: Dairy
Produce Advisory Service of the Milk Marketing Board)

# Danish Apple Cake

METRIC/IMPERIAL
750 g/1½ lb cooking apples
75 g/3 oz butter
75 g/3 oz granulated sugar
100 g/4 oz fresh breadcrumbs
150 ml/¼ pint double cream,
  whipped
redcurrant jelly

AMERICAN
1½ lb cooking apples
6 tablespoons butter
6 tablespoons sugar
2 cups fresh breadcrumbs
⅔ cup heavy cream, whipped
redcurrant jelly

Peel, core and slice the apples. Place in a pan with just enough water to cover and cook, covered, until a pulp. Add 25 g/1 oz/2 tablespoons each of the butter and sugar. Beat well together then allow to cool.

Melt the remaining butter in a large frying pan (skillet). Add the breadcrumbs and remaining sugar and fry together until golden. Allow to cool.

Just before serving, arrange alternate layers of the apple purée and crumbs in a large glass dish, finishing with a layer of crumbs. Lightly whip the cream and spread over the surface. Drizzle the redcurrant jelly over the top to decorate. Serve chilled.
**Serves 4-6**

# French Apple Flan

METRIC/IMPERIAL
1 quantity of shortcrust pastry
  (see page 16)
500 g/1 lb cooking apples
100 g/4 oz golden syrup
2 teaspoons lemon juice
100 g/4 oz apricot jam

AMERICAN
1 quantity of basic pie dough
  (see page 16)
1 lb cooking apples
4 tablespoons maple or light corn
  syrup
2 teaspoons lemon juice
¼ lb apricot jelly

Make up the shortcrust pastry, following the directions on page 16. Roll out and use to line a 20 cm (8 inch) flan tin (pie pan), placed on a baking tray. Bake blind, as for Peachy Meringue Trellis (page 15).

Peel, core and grate half the apples. Mix the grated apples with the syrup and lemon juice, and spread this over the base of the flan case. Peel, core and slice the remaining apples and arrange over the top of the flan. Slightly warm the apricot jam (jelly) then sieve. Brush over the surface of the apples. Bake in a moderate oven (180°C/350°F, Gas Mark 4) for a further 30 to 35 minutes. Serve hot or cold.
**Serves 4-6**

# Gala Ring

**METRIC/IMPERIAL**

**Pastry**
1 quantity of choux pastry
  (see page 80)
vanilla essence (optional)
**Filling**
50 g/2 oz butter or margarine
15 g/½ oz plain flour
200 ml/⅓ pint milk
1 egg, separated
1 tablespoon caster sugar
¼ tablespoon vanilla essence
300 ml/½ pint double cream,
  whipped
225 g/8 oz icing sugar, sifted
1-2 tablespoons water
glacé cherries and angelica

**AMERICAN**

1 quantity of choux pastry
  (see page 80)
vanilla extract (optional)
**Filling**
¼ cup butter or margarine
2 tablespoons flour
⅞ cup milk
1 egg, separated
1 tablespoon sugar
¼ teaspoon vanilla extract
1¼ cups heavy cream, whipped
½ lb confectioners' sugar, sifted
1-2 tablespoons water
candied cherries and angelica

Make up the choux pastry as for the profiterole recipe on page 80, adding the vanilla essence (extract), if liked.

Place the pastry in a piping (pastry) bag fitted with a 2 cm (¾ inch) plain nozzle. Pipe a circle about 15-18 cm (6-7 inch) diameter on a greased baking tray. Bake in a hot oven (220°C/425°F, Gas Mark 7 on the second shelf from the top) for 15 minutes. Reduce the oven temperature to 190°C/375°F, Gas Mark 5 and bake for a further 20 to 25 minutes. Cool.

To make the filling, melt the butter or margarine in a pan. Stir in the flour and cook, stirring constantly, for about 1 minute. Gradually stir in the milk, and bring to the boil, stirring constantly, until the sauce has thickened. Cool slightly then add the egg yolk and sugar. Cool some more and add the vanilla essence (extract) and the whipped cream. Whisk the egg white and fold gently into the mixture.

Split the choux ring in half, scrape out any uncooked dough and fill with the sauce mixture. Beat the icing (confectioners') sugar and water together until smooth and glossy. Carefully pour the icing (frosting) over the ring, allowing it to run down the sides. Decorate with cherries and angelica. Serve cold.
**Serves 4-6**

# Beignets Soufflé

| METRIC/IMPERIAL | AMERICAN |
|---|---|
| **Choux pastry** | **Choux pastry** |
| *65 g/2½ oz plain flour* | *½ cup plus 2 tablespoons* |
| *2 eggs* | *all-purpose flour* |
| *40 g/1½ oz butter* | *2 eggs* |
| *150 ml/¼ pint water* | *3 tablespoons butter* |
| *pinch of salt* | *⅔ cup water* |
| *oil for deep-frying* | *pinch of salt* |
| **To serve** | *oil for deep-frying* |
| *50 g/2 oz caster sugar* | **To serve** |
| *½ teaspoon ground cinnamon* | *¼ cup sugar* |
| | *½ teaspoon ground cinnamon* |

To make the choux pastry, sift the flour on to a large sheet of greaseproof (wax) paper. Beat eggs thoroughly. Place butter, water and salt in a saucepan and bring slowly to the boil. Add the flour all at once and remove the pan from the heat. Beat thoroughly until the mixture leaves the sides of the pan. Add the beaten eggs gradually and beat well until the mixture is smooth and shiny. Heat the oil to 185°C/360°F or until a cube of bread becomes golden in about 20 seconds.

Place the choux mixture in a piping (pastry) bag fitted with a plain 1 cm (½ inch) nozzle. Pipe small rounds of mixture, or place teaspoonsful of mixture into the hot fat and fry for about 5 minutes turning them occasionally. Lift out and drain the beignets soufflés. Dredge with sugar and sprinkle with ground cinnamon. Serve hot.
**Serves 6**

# Zabaglione

| METRIC/IMPERIAL | AMERICAN |
|---|---|
| *4 egg yolks* | *4 egg yolks* |
| *100 g/4 oz caster sugar* | *½ cup sugar* |
| *150 ml/¼ pint Marsala* | *⅔ cup Marsala* |

Place the egg yolks, sugar and Marsala in a heatproof bowl, over a pan of simmering water. Whisk continually until the mixture is thick and foamy. Pour immediately into small individual serving dishes and serve warm, accompanied with sponge finger biscuits (cookies).
**Serves 4**

BEIGNETS SOUFFLÉ *(Photograph: British Egg Information Service)*

# Walnut and Raspberry Roll

| METRIC/IMPERIAL | AMERICAN |
|---|---|
| 4 eggs | 4 eggs |
| 75 g/3 oz caster sugar | 1/3 cup sugar |
| 40 g/1 1/2 oz walnuts, ground | 1/3 cup ground walnuts |
| 40 g/1 1/2 oz plain flour | 6 tablespoons all-purpose flour |
| pinch of ground cinnamon | pinch of ground cinnamon |
| 25 g/1 oz margarine, melted | 2 tablespoons margarine, melted |
| little icing sugar | little confectioners' sugar |
| 450 ml/3/4 pint double cream, whipped | 2 cups heavy cream, whipped |
| little sugar to taste | little sugar to taste |
| 350 g/12 oz raspberries, fresh or frozen (washed and hulled if fresh) | 3/4 lb raspberries, fresh or frozen (washed and hulled if fresh) |

Line a 25 x 30 cm (10 x 12 inch) swiss roll tin (jelly roll pan) with greaseproof (non-stick parchment) paper. Dust lightly with flour.

Whisk the eggs and sugar together until thick and light in colour. Gently fold in the walnuts, flour and cinnamon. Fold in the melted margarine. Carefully spread the mixture evenly over the prepared tin (pan). Bake in a moderately hot oven, (190°C/375°F, Gas Mark 5) for 20 to 25 minutes or until the cake springs back when tested.

Trim away the hard edges of the cake. Turn it out on to a sheet of greaseproof (wax) paper, sprinkled with icing (confectioners') sugar and roll up fairly tightly. Leave to cool.

Sweeten the cream with sugar to taste. Unroll the sponge, and spread 2/3 of the cream over the surface. Top with most of the raspberries, reserving a few of the best for decoration; reroll the sponge. Chill for 30 minutes then place on a serving dish. Cover the entire roll with a thin layer of the remaining cream. Pipe a few whirls down the centre and top with the remaining raspberries. Serve chilled.

**Serves 6–8**

# Strawberry Almond Tart

**METRIC/IMPERIAL**

**Pastry**
*175 g/6 oz plain flour*
*pinch of salt*
*75 g/3 oz margarine*
*50 g/2 oz caster sugar*
*1 egg yolk*
*1 tablespoon water (optional)*

**Filling and Decoration**
*50 g/2 oz margarine*
*100 g/4 oz caster sugar*
*75 g/3 oz cream cheese, softened*
*2 eggs*
*50 g/2 oz plain flour*
*50 g/2 oz ground almonds*
*few drops almond essence*
*1 egg white*
*100 g/4 oz strawberries, washed
  and hulled*
*2 tablespoons redcurrant jelly*

**AMERICAN**

**Pastry**
*1 ½ cups all-purpose flour*
*pinch of salt*
*6 tablespoons margarine*
*¼ cup sugar*
*1 egg yolk*
*1 tablespoon water (optional)*

**Filling and Decoration**
*¼ cup margarine*
*½ cup sugar*
*6 tablespoons cream cheese, softened*
*2 eggs*
*½ cup all-purpose flour*
*½ cup ground almonds*
*few drops almond extract*
*1 egg white*
*¼ lb strawberries, washed and
  hulled*
*2 tablespoons redcurrant jelly*

For the pastry, sift the flour and salt into a bowl. Add the margarine and rub into the flour until the mixture resembles fine breadcrumbs. Add the sugar and the egg yolk and mix until firm, adding the water, if necessary. Knead lightly, then wrap in plastic wrap and rest for about 30 minutes in the refrigerator.

To make the filling, cream the margarine and sugar together until light and fluffy. Gradually beat in the cream cheese and the eggs, one at a time. Finally add the flour, ground almonds and almond essence (extract) to taste. Whisk the egg white and fold in gently.

Roll out the pastry and use to line a 20 cm (8 inch) flan tin (pie pan). Reserve the pastry trimmings. Pour the cheese mixture into the case and decorate with strips of the remaining pastry, lattice fashion. Bake in a moderately hot oven (200°C/400°F, Gas Mark 6) for 35 minutes or until golden brown. Allow to cool. Place the cheesecake on a serving plate and decorate with the strawberries. Brush the strawberries with a little melted redcurrant jelly, and serve the cheesecake cold with pouring cream.

**Serves 6–8**

# French Fruit Tart

METRIC/IMPERIAL
100 g/4 oz plain flour
pinch of salt
50 g/2 oz butter
2 egg yolks
150 g/5 oz caster sugar
75 g/3 oz cream cheese
300 ml/½ pint cooked custard,
  cooled
few drops almond essence
extra sugar
little water
250 g/8 oz plums, halved and
  stoned
redcurrant jelly

AMERICAN
1 cup all-purpose flour
pinch of salt
¼ cup butter
2 egg yolks
⅔ cup sugar
6 tablespoons cream cheese
1¼ cups cooked, custard, cooled
few drops almond extract
extra sugar
little water
½ lb plums, halved and pitted
redcurrant jelly

Sift the flour and salt on to a board. Make a well in the centre and place the butter, egg yolks and 50 g/2 oz/¼ cup of the sugar in the well. Using the fingertips of one hand, gradually work the butter, egg yolks and sugar together until well blended then work in all the flour. Knead lightly then leave to rest for one hour.

Roll out the pastry and use to line a greased 20 cm (8 inch) flan tin (pie pan) placed on a baking tray. Bake blind, following the instructions for Peachy Meringue Trellis (see page 15).

Blend the cream cheese and remaining sugar together. Gradually beat in the custard and almond essence (extract) to taste. Continue beating until the mixture is smooth. Pour the custard mixture over the base of the prepared flan case. Make a sugar syrup, using the sugar and water and poach the plums in this until tender, but still whole. Cool then drain the plums and arrange, cut side down on top of the filling. Brush with a little heated redcurrant jelly and serve cold with pouring cream.
**Serves 4-6**

# SAUCES

## Syrup Cream Sauce

METRIC/IMPERIAL
*50 g/2 oz butter*
*50 g/2 oz icing sugar*
*50 g/2 oz golden syrup*
*2 tablespoons milk*
*few drops almond essence*

AMERICAN
*¼ cup butter*
*½ cup confectioners' sugar*
*¼ cup maple or light corn syrup*
*2 tablespoons milk*
*few drops almond extract*

Cream the butter and sugar until light and fluffy. Beat in the syrup, milk and almond essence (extract) to taste. Chill in the refrigerator until firm. Serve spoonsful over hot baked and steamed puddings or baked apples.
**Serves 4–6**

## Apple and Raspberry Sauce

METRIC/IMPERIAL
*500 g/1 lb cooking apples*
*4 tablespoons raspberry jam*
*1 tablespoon water*
*sugar to taste*

AMERICAN
*1 lb cooking apples*
*4 tablespoons raspberry jelly*
*1 tablespoon water*
*sugar to taste*

Peel, core and chop the apples. Place in a large pan, with the other ingredients. Simmer, covered, until the apples are pulpy; strain. Reheat the sauce and serve hot, poured over ice cream, profiteroles, pies and puddings. Also delicious with baked milk puddings.
**Serves 4–6**

# Coffee Nut Sauce

**METRIC/IMPERIAL**
2 tablespoons golden syrup
2 tablespoons brown sugar
15 g/½ oz butter
2 teaspoons arrowroot
2 tablespoons coffee essence
300 ml/½ pint milk
2 tablespoons coarsely crushed
  peanut brittle

**AMERICAN**
2 tablespoons maple or light corn
  syrup
2 tablespoons brown sugar
1 tablespoon butter
2 teaspoons arrowroot flour
2 tablespoons strong black coffee
1¼ cups milk
2 tablespoons coarsely crushed
  peanut brittle

Bring the syrup, sugar and butter to the boil in a medium pan. Simmer until the mixture turns golden then remove from the heat. Blend the arrowroot, coffee essence (strong black coffee) and milk together and slowly stir in the syrup mixture. Return to the pan and bring back to the boil stirring constantly, until thickened. Add the peanut brittle and serve immediately. Delicious served with ice cream.
**Serves 6**

# Caramel Coffee Sauce

**METRIC/IMPERIAL**
100 g/4 oz butter
100 g/4 oz soft brown sugar
1 tablespoon cornflour
150 ml/¼ pint milk
2 tablespoons coffee essence

**AMERICAN**
½ cup butter
½ cup brown sugar
1 tablespoon cornstarch
⅔ cup milk
2 tablespoons strong black coffee

Melt the butter in a medium pan over a gentle heat. Blend in the sugar and cornflour (cornstarch). Heat until the mixture begins to bubble and thicken, then cook slowly for about 4 minutes, stirring constantly. Remove from the heat and gradually add the milk and coffee essence (strong black coffee). Bring back to the boil then simmer for a further minute. Serve immediately.

Serve with steamed or milk puddings and ice cream.
**Serves 4-6**

# Marshmallow Sauce

METRIC/IMPERIAL
*100 g/4 oz marshmallows*
*2 tablespoons coffee essence*
*1 tablespoon sherry*

AMERICAN
*¼ lb marshmallows*
*2 tablespoons strong black coffee*
*1 tablespoon sherry*

Place all the ingredients in a pan. Heat gently, stirring constantly, until the marshmallows have completely melted. Serve immediately.

Serve hot with ice cream, steamed puddings and fruit desserts.
**Serves 6**


# Lemony Dessert Sauce

METRIC/IMPERIAL
*225 g/8 oz granulated sugar*
*2 tablespoons cornflour or arrowroot*
*pinch of salt*
*120 ml/4 fl oz lemon juice*
*120 ml/4 fl oz water*
*50 g/2 oz butter*
*few drops yellow colouring*
  *(optional)*

AMERICAN
*1 cup sugar*
*2 tablespoons cornstarch or*
  *arrowroot*
*pinch of salt*
*½ cup lemon juice*
*½ cup water*
*¼ cup butter*
*few drops yellow coloring*
  *(optional)*

Place the sugar, cornflour (cornstarch) or arrowroot and salt in a small pan. Blend in the lemon juice and water. Bring to the boil, stirring constantly. Add the butter and continue to cook for a further 5 minutes or until the sauce becomes thick and clear. Add a few drops of colouring to give a pleasant yellow colour, if liked.

Serve the sauce warm over sliced bananas, melon balls, gingerbread, steamed sponge puddings and ice cream.
**Serves 4**

# Chocolate Sauce

| METRIC/IMPERIAL | AMERICAN |
|---|---|
| 75 g/3 oz caster sugar | 6 tablespoons sugar |
| 75 g/3 oz soft brown sugar | 1/2 cup brown sugar |
| 75 g/3 oz cocoa powder | 3/4 cup unsweetened cocoa |
| 300 ml/1/2 pint milk | 1 1/4 cups milk |
| 1 teaspoon vanilla essence | 1 teaspoon vanilla extract |
| 25 g/1 oz butter | 2 tablespoons butter |

Place all the ingredients in a medium pan. Heat gently, stirring, until the sugars have melted and all the ingredients are thoroughly blended. Bring slowly to the boil, then boil briskly for about 2 minutes. Serve hot or cold.

Delicious poured over profiteroles, ice creams and steamed or baked sponge puddings.

**Serves 4-6**

# Custard Sauce

| METRIC/IMPERIAL | AMERICAN |
|---|---|
| 2 eggs | 2 eggs |
| 300 ml/1/2 pint milk | 1 1/4 cups milk |
| 15 g/1/2 oz caster sugar | 1 tablespoon sugar |
| few drops vanilla essence | few drops vanilla extract |

Whisk the eggs together in a basin. Heat the milk, to scalding point and pour on to the eggs. Strain the egg mixture into a heatproof basin and place the basin over a pan of simmering water. Stir the custard until it has thickened and is pale and creamy. Stir in the sugar and vanilla essence (extract) to taste. Serve hot or cold.

Note: If there are egg yolks in the refrigerator, this sauce may be made using leftover egg yolks. Use 3 egg yolks instead of the 2 whole eggs and proceed in the same way.

**Serves 4**

# INDEX

# INDEX

PDO 79-414